A GARLAND SERIES

THE ENGLISH
WORKING CLASS

A Collection of
Thirty Important Titles
That Document and Analyze
Working-Class Life before
the First World War

Edited by

STANDISH MEACHAM
University of Texas

Domestic Service

C. V. Butler

Garland Publishing, Inc.
New York & London
1980

For a complete list of the titles in this series,
see the final pages of this volume.

The volumes in this series are printed on acid-free,
250-year-life paper.

This facsimile has been made from a copy in
the Library of Congress.

Library of Congress Cataloging in Publication Data

Butler, C   Violet.
Domestic service.

(The English working class)
Reprint of the 1916 ed. published by G. Bell, London.
Bibliography: p.
1. Women servants—Great Britain.   I. Title.
II. Series: English working class.
HD6072.G7B87   1980   331.4'8164046'0941   79-56953
ISBN 0-8240-0107-9

Printed in the United States of America

DOMESTIC SERVICE

DOMESTIC SERVICE

AN ENQUIRY BY THE WOMEN'S INDUSTRIAL COUNCIL

REPORT BY

C. V. BUTLER

WITH A SUPPLEMENTARY CHAPTER BY

LADY WILLOUGHBY DE BROKE

LONDON
G. BELL AND SONS, LTD.
1916

THE LONDON AND NORWICH PRESS LIMITED, LONDON AND NORWICH ENGLAND

PREFACE

THIS enquiry was concluded, and the report on it was almost completed, before the war. Various causes have since delayed its publication ; the subject matter, however, has not been much affected. A considerable number of the servant-keeping classes have in the last eighteen months done strenuous manual work in hospitals and canteens ; they may have revised their previous views as to domestic service. During the first two months of the war many servants were dismissed, and there was a temporary over-supply of under-housemaids and lady's maids. Munition work and other new occupations for women have absorbed all this over-supply, except in the case of a few upper servants, and have made the shortage of servants more acute even than before.

This may be some justification for offering an analysis, such as follows, of a number of comparatively small personal difficulties. "And common was the commonplace." The troubles and pleasures of one industrial section, which, through no fault of its own, offers no direct contribution to "war work," seem wholly out of keeping with present problems and anxieties. And yet the conditions of women's labour, in which domestic service still probably represents the largest single section, is not the least of the problems which have developed since August, 1914, and which will come back to us with greater weight after the war.

The method of the enquiry was as follows : Two schedules were drawn up by a committee of the Women's Industrial Council, one in the form of a series of leading statements to be discussed on paper by employers, one consisting of a series of brief questions with spaces for replies and suggestions by servants. Specimens of these are given in Appendix viii.

The former schedule was sent to large numbers of employers in all parts of the British Isles, some copies to members of the Women's Industrial Council and persons known to them, some to addresses received in response to statements and correspondence in the press, some to persons connected with different organisations of women. Special efforts were made to secure replies from employers of different classes and types.

The servants' questionnaire was sent out in the same way. In almost every case the writer sent her name and address (though not for publication), and a large proportion of the answers were long and careful and eminently human documents.

708 replies were received on the employers' schedules, and 566 on those of the servants. Beside these some hundreds of letters were received, either privately or through the press, from employers and workers.

The report has been compiled almost entirely from the material so collected ; the compiler had not taken part in the preliminary enquiry. The result represents not a statistical record, but an attempt to weigh impartially some hundreds of frequently conflicting accounts and opinions. The appendix on training for domestic service is the result of an independent enquiry, supplemented by investigations carried out by the Education Committee of the Women's Industrial Council.

The thanks of the Council are due to the Domestic Servants' Insurance Society, which kindly allowed some hundreds of forms to be distributed through its agency to its members ; to Miss M. S. Barton and Mrs. Bernard Drake, who, as Hon. Secretary to the Committee which undertook the investigation, bore almost the whole burden of the Enquiry ; to Miss M. G. Skinner, Miss W. Rintoul, Miss Catherine Webb and Mrs. H. G. Hale, who spent much time in examining, collecting and sorting the rather unwieldy material ; to Mrs. John M. Hunt, Mrs. Percy Abbott, Councillor George Deighton, Miss L. K. Yates, who gave valuable information based on their expert knowledge ; to various ladies who devoted an immense amount of time to the labour of copying out the voluminous returns ; and perhaps most of all to the large numbers, both of servants and mistresses, who took the trouble to reply at great length and with singular candour.

C. V. BUTLER.

CONTENTS

CONTENTS

APPENDICES—

DOMESTIC SERVICE

INTRODUCTION

According to the Census of 1911, there were in England and Wales 1,359,359 women and girls as well as 54,260 men and boys engaged in indoor domestic service, which was thus the largest form of employment in the country. How far are the conditions in this industry satisfactory ?

It was with no desire to manufacture grievances that the Women's Industrial Council set out, by methods explained in the preface, to gather the views of typical employers and servants on this question. Some of the mistresses and maids circularised by the Council replied virtually that there was no problem of domestic service. " I am always happy. I think domestic service is the best for any girl," wrote one cook-general of twenty-five ; " I consider service is quite the best thing for a steady, respectable girl, and should like all my young relations to enter a gentleman's house," replied a middle-aged nurse with good wages. " I have never had any difficulty with servants ; I try to make them happy and they never leave me ; we feel each other to be friends," wrote, in effect, numbers of employers. And every reader will be able to produce similar instances of contentment. But these represent, we fear, the exceptions, numerous but in the minority. It is a commonplace that the employer, especially the middle-class and small employer, often has great difficulty in finding servants, and that when found, these are apt to be unsatisfactory ; while on the other hand, many servants (not necessarily incompetent), find it hard to get " good " places, and urge their young friends to take up other work. The flood of correspondence that bursts forth whenever the subject is broached in the newspapers shows that all is not well. Discussion of the " servant problem " is indeed apt to become trivial, partly owing to the way in which it has been traditionally treated on the stage and in print, partly owing to the very natural habit among aggrieved parties of insisting on their own private troubles. There is the girl who says that her great objection to service is that she has to address the baby of the house as " master " or " miss " ; and there is the mistress who denounces modern education because her young maid has forgotten to bring in small plates for the second course at lunch. It was with no desire to evoke personal accusations but in the hope of analysing the genuine difficulties, that the Women's Industrial Council undertook its enquiry. For between the violent malcontents who have suffered from exceptionally bad mistresses or maids, and the type which is " always happy " and aloof from the path of reform, there is a very large class whose relationship is not satisfactory and whose mutual jars are partly responsible for the constant undersupply of servants.

In normal circumstances economic pressure fairly well adjusts the supply of labour to the demand for it, and, when an industry is in a satisfactory condition it produces the quality which is more or less up to the standard required. Why has competition not brought this about with regard to domestic service ? " Working-class girls think themselves too fine for such work now," complains the kindly, conservative mistress. " Girls nowadays don't know what is best for them," laments the " old-fashioned maid," or the mother who was once in good service herself. But there must be some better reason than social prejudice to account for the chronic shortage of labour in almost all branches of " Service."

What then are the causes of friction ? They are (1) personal and (2) industrial, to use a distinction which can never be quite complete. The problem is, indeed, not a plain and simple one ; it is only on broad lines that the difficulties of service present themselves alike to the housekeeper in a big establishment, to the much-beloved " family servant," and to the little general, newly sent out from an industrial school or training-home. It varies with different districts of the British Isles, and with the social class from which employer and employed are drawn. It is nothing new for friction to arise between the employer and his personal servant, for it has been reported since the time of the Pharaohs and before. But it has become more acute in the last twenty or thirty years, partly owing to the changed standard of education, which has advanced much more rapidly than the science of household organisation ; partly owing to the increase of wealth and the increased demand for servants ; partly owing to the multiplication of other openings for women's work. In the face of the persuasion of teachers and mothers and outside " social superiors " the most promising girls are apt to prefer lower wages, less material comfort, and much less security of employment in shop or office or factory work, to the often-quoted advantages of domestic service. Most private employers on the other hand think that they give their servants at least as good treatment as that which produced contentment in the time of their own parents, together with much higher wages, and yet they do not get a satisfactory return.

Although domestic servants often speak sadly of them-selves as a class apart, they are by no means cut off from the remainder of the industrial community. The fathers and brothers of many of them have been on strike in recent years, and they have read the newspapers. Industrial unrest and the waves of the suffrage agitation have reached the minds of those servants who think, and have helped to focus the resentment of those who have only room in their minds for their own grievances. Hence the virulent denunciations of domestic service which sometimes fall from those employed in it, and, we may add, from those for whom they work. And yet the great majority of mistresses and servants, once free from their immediate grievances, seem to feel more bewilderment than bitterness over the unsatisfactory conditions which they admit to exist.

The servant question opens the problem of the relation of employer and employed in its most intimate form. Here, if anywhere, it ought to be possible to make one section of the industrial system work smoothly. Domestic service is unique as a calling, because the personal considerations involved are so all-important, and because the employer of such labour does not hire it to produce goods for sale in a fiercely competitive market. Yet it cannot be regarded quite apart from other forms of wage-earning labour. It is because its difficulties are both like and unlike those of industry as a whole, that some really original treatment of them should be possible. The future of domestic service is primarily, though not exclusively, a woman's question ; and it deserves really careful thought and constructive treatment. This is the more worth while because there are so many available object-lessons to show how entirely satisfactory domestic service can be, in spite of all possible drawbacks. To quote again—

From a mistress :

" My experience in keeping house for fifty-six years is that I have never had the least difficulty—in a family of fairly good means, though not rich—in getting good servants or in contenting them and making them happy."

From a retired servant, after forty-three years' service :

" I cannot speak too highly of service. If I had my time over again I would go to service again ; I have always been treated very kind indeed."

These are the sort of experiences we should all like to see multiplied, even though we might wish the conditions changed in detail.

As far as possible, employers and employed will, in this report, speak for themselves on the personal and the industrial aspects of the problem.

Under the first heading the personal drawbacks most often urged against service, both by employers and servants and their relatives, will be considered : the lack of liberty, of companionship and of outside interests, together with the loss of caste which it is said to involve.

The industrial aspects of domestic service will be next considered—its organisation, standard of efficiency and its wage-earning power, together with its prospects. The differences between domestic and other sorts of work will be analysed, and it is hoped that the result of these investigations may lead to practical recommendations for the future.

PART ONE

THE PERSONAL ASPECT

(i.) LIBERTY.—Almost all servants, whether they are personally contented or discontented, agree that lack of liberty is the dominant cause of the unpopularity of service, in so far as such unpopularity exists. Most of the employing class would agree in this, though many of those who are most genuinely interested in the welfare of their juniors, apart from the question of their class in life, would say that such loss of liberty may be very wholesome. One manager of a girls' club wrote that it is often good in her opinion to send a young girl even from a happy home into service, because she learns self-dependence and the habit of discipline, just as the home-taught daughter of richer parents generally gains by going to a boarding school. Many of the older servants agree in this, one saying with probable truth that—unfortunately—it is generally not the best, but the second rate servants who at present " stand out for their liberty."

Wholesome though the lack of liberty may be from the ascetic point of view, yet it stands out as the chief drawback to service, at least in the opinion of many girls and their friends in " business." Liberty may, as history has shown, be interpreted to mean almost anything from mere absence of definite restraint to the possibility of free self-development. For the domestic worker its loss is summed up in the often-repeated phrase that " service is such a tie."

This may be the preliminary to complaints of definite restrictions as to churchgoing or about details of dress, such as the wearing of a particular shape of cap indoors

13

or of bonnet out of doors ; it may refer to rules about
the servants' use of leisure or methods of address ; or about
asking leave before going out on a small necessary errand ;
or it may extend to restrictions on " freedom of thought "
and of friendships. But more important than these
specific causes of complaint, which would never occur in
many households, there is the feeling of being under
orders all day, of being never " off duty," which is repeated
wearily by many servants who have kept their places for
years, think well of their employers, and do not complain
of actual overwork. It is to shake off this feeling that the
demand for a recognized time of freedom daily, be it
half an hour or two or three hours, is growing. This would
be the chief justification of widespread daily service, the
pros and cons of which we shall consider later. A number
of overwrought servants, especially cooks and parlourmaids, have written to say what a relief they find it now
to have daily work only, so that they get a complete
change of thought at night, tiring though the walk home
may be.

As a matter of fact, many servants have at intervals a
great deal of liberty, too much for some inexperienced
girls. A lady with many years' knowledge of servants, as
mistress and friend, writes that most of those with whom
she, as the head of local branches of the Girls' Friendly
Society and Young Women's Christian Association, comes
into contact have free time, very frequently from 3 to
10 p.m. at least twice a week. " We have opened a rest
room for them because they are out so much. For those
not so cared for, independence may have many dangers."
Many servants and workers among young women would
be able from their own experience to produce instances of
the bad effects of too much " liberty " upon the girl who,
by reaction from restriction on the other days of the week,
makes up her mind to have a " real good time " on her
nights out. It is the fear of this that causes some careful
mistresses to think that a weekly attendance at church and
possibly at a bible-class, are the only ways in which a girl
of sixteen can safely be allowed to spend her time outside
her mistress' house. The prevalence of these two extremes
just shows how difficult it is to hit the happy mean, and

how hard it is to prescribe for a body so widely different
in age, temperament, social standing and outlook, as that
of domestic servants.

Lack of liberty, however, remains the expressed or
unexpressed grievance in the majority of cases. To some
extent it is inherent in domestic service, and is a necessary
exchange for the greater comfort obtainable and for the
sheltered life. It is for the individual to estimate the
value of the exchange. The restrictions involved in service
are in no sense new, but they are probably felt more than
they were fifty years ago, because of the greater lack of
home discipline and of the increased chances of amusement. " Girls are thrown into service anyhow at fifteen
or sixteen, after never being made to do as they are told
at home, and of course they find it hard," as an upper
servant wrote. It is also probably accentuated by the
conservatism of our home life. " Fifty years ago the
servant girl had much more liberty than her employer's
daughter, now the reverse is the case." Restrictions are,
of course, necessary as much in the interests of the servant
as of the mistress ; and good servants like other reasonable people do not resent but appreciate some measure of
restraint. Curtailments on freedom are often due, as many
servants and mistresses agree, to its abuse by bad servants
who " spoil places for good maids." But admitting all
this, it would be well if employers would realise much
more widely than at present that the standard of living,
and with it the interpretation of " discipline," have changed,
so that desire for liberty is not necessarily a demand for
licence ; also that it answers better on the whole to have
a very few strict rules and beyond these to trust servants,
and that such treatment fits in best with the spirit of the
age. This makes a much greater demand on the employer's
discretion and tact than a policy of restriction. " There
is a grave need for instruction to mistresses how to manage
servants "—writes a lady after forty-two years' experience
of prosperous housekeeping.

It is impossible to do more than produce loose generalisa-
tions on this aspect of the servant problem, because its
treatment must depend on circumstances ; but all who wish
to improve the conditions of service should keep the

desire for liberty in mind, as the fundamental need behind
any specific reforms.

Below are given a few typical expressions of the desire
for greater freedom, and some comparisons, on the score
of liberty, between domestic service, shop and factory
work.

" The chief improvement needed in domestic service is :—Freedom
(in actions and thought) whether on religious matters or on views
on politics if any, and that it should not be against them ; also more
freedom for outdoor exercise and the freedom of using the time as
their own.

" There are several things that could be done to make domestic
service more pleasant. First of all if more freedom were given
girls would take more interest in their work. Speaking of myself,
I am very often shut right indoors from one week to another,
Tuesday to Tuesday I never have a day out ; my mistress will not
be inconvenienced so far. I consider all maids should have two hours
each day to call their own, with the option of going out or remaining
in the house, but in any case the time to be their own. Domestic
service would not be nearly such a monotonous occupation if a little
variation were included. A good home and good food *is not all* that
is required by servants."

" I have tried to fill this form up to the best of my ability : of
course I have always worked in the hat works, and we know all the
dread girls have of losing their liberty ; one girl I know here went
to service, her eyes were too weak for our work, but she is coming
back ; she is so lonely and missed her evenings out ; she is steady,
over thirty years of age, but they watch her and only allow one
half-day per week and the change is too much. I was in a sanatorium
in the South a short time ago, and met several servants there, and
really those in good families had a splendid time, in a great many
respects, but they have not the same independent outlook on life
you meet among girls in workshops, and where men are concerned,
they gave me the impression that domestic service does not improve
the morality of the girl : I suppose it is because of the repression.
Of course in the North it is a difficult thing to get good servants ;
our girls are too independent, I suppose, but after all it is so much
the better for the mistress if she has a maid who can think for herself
and take care of herself, and realises that really she is doing good
work in doing household work. Our girls, although they know that
the servant is better paid as a rule, prefer their liberty ; they would
not mind if they were allowed out when they had finished the main
portion of their work ; it could be so arranged that they could have
two or three hours' liberty during the evenings."

" Servants should have say one-and-a-half to two hours off every
day for recreation, where they live in. Factory workers at fourteen
years start with 6s. in Leek. Girls here leave service regularly to

come into the factory and very rarely go back. Wages are better, hours shorter, and work much easier. Servants seem to lose their independence while in service and regain it in the factory. That is due to organisation. I have worked in the factory since I was ten, with six months' children's nursing between, that is twenty years in all, so I can speak from experience as to the advantages of the factory. Factory life is not pleasant by any means, but the freedom and knowing when you have finished work is worth a good deal to a girl. The uniform, especially the cap, is looked upon as a mark of servitude, which a girl of an independent nature resents. Hence the girls prefer the factory."

A cook-housekeeper, with thirty-one years' experience of service—started at fourteen :

" I always wished to go to service, and as my parents were poor, I was obliged to go, as they had no money to spare to educate me for anything else. I will never regret being a domestic servant. I have tried to do my duty well, and have been well rewarded for doing so. I consider that we are better off than shop-girls or factory girls : we may not have so much money for wages, but we have our board and lodging free, also washing, which is equal to 12s. or 14s. a week. When the shop or factory girl pays for her food and lodgings she has very little. If a girl is not well trained at home she will never make a good servant : girls now-a-days are spoiled at home ; their mothers never teach them how to work."

A cook-general at £25. Started from the country at fourteen, now fifty-seven :

" I should not have gone to service could I have kept out of it at all, only my dear mother was a widow and I had to do something. . . . I did try to learn the tailoring, but sitting did not agree with me, so mother put me to service. . . . One thing I will own in Domestic Service, it is the best thing for paying, as you are sure of your food and lodgings and washing . . . but none the more for that, I would not stay in it another day could I do anything else. As a child when my school-fellows were talking about what they should do when grown up, I used to say I hoped my mother would never put me to service."

(ii.) COMPANIONSHIP.—It is possible to suffer equally from uncongenial neighbours and from loneliness, and the question of companionship so far as it concerns working hours obviously affects different classes of servants quite differently. In the case of the general, it is sheer lack of company that is the drawback. Of course, not all single-handed servants feel this. Several general servants with a good deal of free time and independent interests,

B

went out of their way in their replies to the Council's
enquiry to say that they were very happy and greatly
preferred solitary service to their former experiences as
members of large households. And under working-class
mistresses in whose houses the young maid shares her
meals with the family, and perhaps sleeps with one of the
children, or in the case of older self-dependent women, the
difficulty of indoor companionship does not exist. But
loneliness is often a very real trial in the life of the young
servant, the strictly kept between-maid in a household of
middle-aged maids, or the young girl who first goes out,
as the great majority of servants do, into small houses
where no other maids are kept.   One correspondent sent
a vivid description of a recent debate in a girls' club on
the well-worn topic of domestic service versus shop and
factory work. The girls were by no means unanimous,
but the opponents of service waxed eloquent on the
dreariness of lonely vigils by young maids waiting up for
their employers' return from late evening festivities, and
on the lack of change from dealing with an exigent
mistress.   Other maids who wrote gave instances of young
girls known to them being left all alone to take care of
the suburban villa of their employers, while the latter
took their fortnight or three weeks' holiday. It seems
hardly necessary to comment on the folly of this, which
any rescue worker will confirm. But apart from such
extremes, the loneliness at meals and work and recreation
would make it generally undesirable, if it could be avoided,
for the very young to begin as general servants. It is
another matter if the working mistress is at her best or
the employer kindly enough to take trouble to be really
sympathetic with the young maid's interests. A number
of elder servants commented on this, and recommended that
the young girl should either start under a good working
mistress, or preferably in a good sized household where
the elder servants would take pains to train her. Unfortunately, this is a counsel of perfection. Under present
conditions of entry into service, only a very small minority
of girls can go straight from school into a household with
several servants, and their lot is not always very enviable
when they do so. For the rest, we all know instances of

the homesickness of little girls from large families, when
expected to work and eat and sleep alone, as soon as they
go out to service.   Modern working-class children are
forced to be gregarious ; they are bound to spend five hours
a day with other children during school sessions almost
from the time that they can walk, while voluntary clubs
and guilds bring them together again out of school, for a
further corporate existence.   By day and night equally
they are hardly ever without companions.   The tendency
of their whole training is against a single-handed existence,
and the strain of solitude in their first places may be very
great.   This is a psychological trial that kindness and
commonsense on the part of the mistress can obviously
minimise.   But unfortunately it seems still necessary to repeat the need for even such moderate use of imagination.

In a large household the difficulty of loneliness disappears,
—and therefore employers of many servants meet with
them more easily.   To this the head of one of the best
known registries in the kingdom bears witness, saying that
it is in only one or two special classes of work, such as that
of laundry-maids, that there is any difficulty at all in filling
these vacancies.

A very sensible suggestion was made by a housekeeper
who wrote from a castle, that the mistress, or the person
responsible for the management of the household, should
take pains to grade the servants carefully ; i.e., that she
should engage upper and under servants respectively of
much the same ages, so that they might fall into natural
groups.   Otherwise the young servant may feel very
friendless even among numbers.

Outside the big households and the single servant places,
come all the two, three, and four servant houses, which
produce probably the happiest form of domestic service.
Any difficulty here comes from the lack of congenial company, not from solitude.   Hence the saying of one cheery
young woman that general service is best, as " You can't
fall out with yourself."   A number of " good " servants
complain how dreadful it is to share a room with " some
low-class woman " who perhaps drinks, unknown to her
employer.   Most agree that it is much more from each other
than from their employers that servants suffer.   Of course,

as some hundreds of mistresses pointed out, in no rank of life can people choose their fellow-workers. A youngster's life in the workshop can be made almost unbearable by his foreman, and there can be few workrooms without their quarrels. But outside domestic service, the workers are not compelled to spend together almost the whole of the non-working, as well as the working-hours. They go back to homes which, whatever their defects and however they may criticise their members in private life, will almost invariably support them through thick and thin against the outside world. Hence the desirability that the mistress, for the servant's sake and her own, should bear this question of congeniality in mind. And she cannot do this unless she takes the trouble—often it means a great deal of trouble —to know her servants and abstain from treating them as machines. Hence also the importance of realising their desire for greater freedom. Servants' quarrels would be much less common if they had more fresh air and access to outside interests.

Ingenuity in this direction would do much to lessen the difficulties of the servant problem in the country. The mistress of a large household in North Wales wrote : " I get over the difficulty by keeping my servants supplied with books, work, and games and by letting them use the motor for expeditions as often as possible." All mistresses of country households cannot rise to this level of considera- tion, but it may at least suggest a standard.

In towns, the problem equally of loneliness and of uncongenial companionship could be solved to a certain extent by the organization of competent daily servants, and the establishment of servants' hostels. These would not, probably, at first meet a very wide-spread demand ; but it is clear that there are a number of " experienced " servants, who, after a time, would thankfully escape either from the loneliness of single-servant life, or the close companionship which years of residential service had made irksome. And there is a new type of busy master and mistress who would be glad to accept the possibility of engaging houseworkers by the day or hour, and thus avoid the responsibility of condemning the one servant to hours of unnatural solitude, or of forcing the maids into a companionship which produces constant quarrels. There are many people in all classes to whom life in a close community is, or becomes, unbearable. This obviously opens up a field for the organiser who combines business capacity with a power of sympathetic understanding of the desires of the social classes which supply and demand servants.

An intelligent cook who married at about thirty, wrote from her husband's shack in Western Canada :

" There must be unity between fellow-servants to make a happy home. One disagreeable fellow-servant makes an unhappiness, which causes a lot of misery that could be avoided, and unity gains many friends. I know some friends who have been in the same situation for years ; they work together, and if one goes out, the other two do her work. The lady never asks where they have been, but is kind and considerate for them. When one marries another friend is ready to go there, and they never leave unless it is to be married. . . . I am sure it does not altogether rest with the ladies ; one disagreeable fellow-servant can make a whole household unhappy, as I can say from experience, but some of my best friends are late fellow servants."

The vexed question of servants' visitors comes in here. On no subject was such divergence of opinions and custom shown in the replies. A large number of mistresses said that they always allowed their maids to have women visitors either when they liked (for they could trust them), or whenever leave was asked ; or to one fixed meal per week. A small number said that they made no restrictions at all about visitors of any kind. Many again said that they had granted such freedom, but had been forced to withdraw it because it caused friction among servants themselves ; because servants asked unsuitable persons to the house ; because they really could not afford the constant meals supplied by the servants to their visitors. The latter is indeed a case often quoted by the maids themselves, where bad servants spoil conditions for their successors.

As a whole, the mistresses clearly wanted to let their servants receive their friends, though they found it very difficult to do so. This was one of the subjects raised by the Council which had obviously received the most sympathetic consideration. But the hard employer, who does exist, was scarcely touched by the Council's enquiry.

Almost but not quite all the maids said strongly that they would like to be allowed to have their friends to see them. They said how dreadful it was to be shut in from one Thursday to another—and perhaps miss your afternoon out when it came, and never to be allowed openly to have any outsider to speak to you, not even your own sister from the villa in the next street. An organised body of servants replied :—" Service is like prison. Seeing that the employer's house, where the servant ' lives in ' is her home, she should have practically the same liberty to invite friends and relations there as she would have to her parents' home. If she is not to be trusted not to abuse this privilege, don't employ her."

It is generally about women visitors that these open-minded discussions turn. The question of allowing men " friends " to call is one which has exercised the mind of many a careful mistress. On the one hand she may feel that she stands in *loco parentis* to a young maid away from home, and that she is responsible both for the girl's chance of making a happy marriage and for her safety meanwhile ; generally such a mistress will find out about the young man and allow him, under restrictions, to come to the house if he wishes to do so, realising that the restrictions of service may in any case prevent men of the same social class meeting and pursuing the acquaintance, especially of the " upper-class " servant. Busy or careless mistresses on the other hand are apt to dislike the idea of a strange young man being below stairs, and fall back on the formula " no followers allowed." A number of girls said it was quite impossible to get to know your " friend " if you only saw him in the street once a fortnight, while the members of a young men's club, when consulted, said just the same. We give some rather naïve expressions of opinion :—

A young house-parlourmaid from a suburban rectory, writes :

" A good many mistresses object to men friends, why, I don't know, they forget they must have had them, for them to have married. Could not one day, say once a month, be set aside for friends of either sex to come and visit servants, particularly when servants are far away from their gentlemen friends, and only see them once a month or fortnight, and it is not always easy for both to get out at the same time ? I live away from my friend and only see him once a fortnight, but my mistress allowed me to change my time out so as to make it that we both get out. But all mistresses would not do that. I have refused places because of afternoons out, and one lady even went so far as to say that she could not engage me, as no followers were allowed, simply because I was engaged to a young man. If mistresses allowed maids a little more freedom, and they were not made to feel that they were tied so much, and so much of a servant, they would find girls do more and serve them better."

A hard-worked housemaid, now earning £24 :

" A great thing against domestic service is the rule, ' no followers allowed.' Ladies are quite right in not allowing young men to their houses whom they know nothing about, but supposing a girl has been keeping company with a young man whom she can only see for a few hours three times a fortnight, that is, alternate Sundays and one evening a week, what can she know of his habits, likes and dislikes in home life, if she only sees him when he puts on his best manners. He might be entirely different from what one judges him to be ; and if they should marry it might lead to unhappiness and disappointment. If ladies are doubtful about their maids' sweethearts, they could enquire about their characters at their employers'. There are many ways in which they could find out if a young man is honest or not."

A further problem of domestic service is the question of companionship out of doors. All the servants circularised were asked :—" Can you spend your free time at a club ? " Only a small proportion replied to the question, because as they belonged to no clubs they evidently felt that it did not concern them. Of those who answered, most said that they only had time in their much too short evenings to go to church, or to shop. Only twenty per cent. of those who filled in the Council's forms belonged or had belonged to the Girls' Friendly Society and the Young Women's Christian Association ; twenty-five per cent. in all belonged or had belonged to a club or organisation of some kind before the passing of the National Health Insurance Act, but more than one-third of these said they had given up their membership because they were never sure enough of their time off to attend the lodge or take part in its social life. A few, however, expressed the greatest gratitude for their membership of these societies, and a few others expressed a great desire to know of a club which they might attend.

Many of those circularised had recently made their first experience of corporate life by joining a Friendly Society under the Insurance Act, and did not at the time respond to the idea of further common action, compulsory or voluntary.

There is, however, a decided scope for further well-managed clubs for servants, and this in spite of the fact that many kindly-designed servants' clubs have failed. There is room for many more up-to-date clubs managed on Girls' Friendly Society and Young Women's Christian Association lines, such as those which have already done so well in many towns. The more these can be left to the members themselves to manage the better, though many unsophisticated servants will greatly prefer to be ": managed for " by kindly friends at their club or guild and will be much the better for this. Others might like a club room to which they could bring their friends, men or women, and give them well-served, cheap meals. One such club has been worked with great success at a Girls' Friendly Society Lodge. Such clubs would obviate the difficulty of bringing a young man to the employer's house, and would also occupy some long wet Sunday evenings, which cannot be filled completely by the most regular church-goer. On week-days a good many girls said that they liked best to stay out in the fresh air. The difficulty is indeed lessened by the habit among servants of taking places near their homes, and probably the more they do this when they are young the better, if their homes are good. But the country girls and adventurous spirits go long distances ; they are not all members of societies, nor do they necessarily find them congenial, and there are still frequent, well-authenticated stories of young and friendless servants being locked out by their employers to walk about the Sunday streets from 3 to 10 or 11 p.m. Surely there is room for new and very careful efforts in this direction ? Unless the clubs are grouped round insurance societies, they need not necessarily be established for servants as such ; ideally it would be better for them to meet people in other occupations (as many mistresses took care to point out).

A mistress writes :

" I approve strongly of the suggestion that social clubs should be available for servants, but I think it would be much better not to have the membership confined to the servant class : I know one club where my servants go where they meet all classes—small tradesmen, Corporation employees, etc., etc. It is a very great success, and generally two of my servants go about once a week : I hardly ever know which of them is going and always find the work, whether waiting at table or cooking the dinner, satisfactorily performed by the other two. My servants have perfect liberty to ask any of their relations, friends or young men to tea or supper, and I have never found this abused."

If the work of establishing clubs of any description is to be done at all, it must be really well done, with consideration of what modern girls and young women want and need. The initiative will probably have to be taken from outside, for servants have little idea of, or opportunity for common action. Such a movement would be not so much in the interests of the " old-fashioned " servant as in those of recent recruits and the next generation. It will be the more desirable if, as is to be hoped, servants in the future do have more leisure than at present. Any measure of the sort would have to be taken with full consideration of local conditions, of the prevailing types of servant and existing provision for them. Probably all that is wanted in many towns is a development, on rather more up-to-date lines, of what is already being done by the Girls' Friendly Society and Young Women's Christian Association ; while elsewhere, especially in London, there would be opportunities for self-governing clubs, managed, if not promoted, by servants themselves.

As a whole, then, among the mistresses and maids who wrote to the Women's Industrial Council, there was a general feeling that lack of companionship, or lack of congenial companionship, was one of the great drawbacks of service as compared with other occupations, especially among the very young and the middle-aged workers. To a certain extent this was felt to be inevitable. To a much larger extent it was thought to be remediable.[1]

(iii.) INTERESTS.—A servant's life, even if comfortable, is apt to be very limited in its outlook, and a great number of the replies received from servants show that they are

[1] The replies summarised in Appendix vii to questions on the position of the hotel servant, illustrate for better or worse the common desire for companionship and variety, and the comparative popularity of a form of service which offers these.

conscious of this and regret it.   At present this feeling
often expresses itself merely in discontent, so that good
mistresses sometimes look back upon the generation just
before the era of compulsory education as the golden age
of mistress and maid. The lady whose comment on
present conditions of service is here given will probably
find many to agree with her.

" I have been a mistress for twenty years, and owing to a
roving life with the army, have employed the most varied national-
ities—Spanish, Maltese, Italians, South Africans (Blacks) and more
lately, French, Italian and Swiss.   I do not hesitate to say that for
middle class servants—not the highly trained butler, footman, lady's
maid, etc., of English rich households—I have invariably found
that the more education the worse the servant. . . . The totally
uneducated Italian and Maltese were the *best*, the happiest and most
contented, and the French peasant type the next.   I consider the
Council education has ruined girls for service, and caused them to be
ambitious beyond their capabilities, looking down upon domestic
work when they have no qualification for any other work or profession.   I would suggest that quite half the girl's school life should be
solely occupied with domestic training, and that some system of
apprenticing girls to good housekeepers might be practicable.   In
England I never engage a woman under forty, as I find girls discontented, delicate and lazy.   My servants *never* leave, so I cannot be a
hard mistress."

But for better or worse (surely for better) modern
elementary education aims at the all-round development
of the pupils of the State.   If it has not yet nearly reached
its ideal, we may hope that it will do so more not less
closely than at present, while access to good literature and
music, and opportunities of travel and recreation and the
exercise of responsibility are multiplied.   At present
servants, as a class, and other manual workers, have both
too little leisure and too little training in the right use of
what they have.

Admitting then the prevalence of the half-conscious
desire for self-development, how does it affect servants ?
It must be agreed that under any circumstances the
middle class servant often lives an artificial life, remote
from the interests and give and take of family life.   Three
or four women living, working, eating and sleeping in the
same house, with not more than a fortnight's break in the
year, are almost certain to become narrow-minded, whether

they are servants or not. Still more is this the case in the two or one servant households.

Two-thirds of all those circularised who replied said virtually—

Service is dull for the servant :

It makes her seem dull to other people.

They then described the different directions in which they would like to expand. Extracts from their replies illustrate this better than any summary could do.

The first is from a general servant, a member of the Salvation Army, aged twenty-six, who entered service because she was " anxious to leave home," and found this the only means of employment in which she could be independent from the beginning. She writes that she would not advise a young friend to enter service—

" Because service on the whole is very limited, and it is only in exceptional circumstances that people obtain a fair amount of freedom. Because on the other hand, you have a much larger sphere and opportunities of making a position outside domestic service. Every servant should have a certain amount of free time off daily, and work should be finished by a stipulated time in the evenings ; after that the individual should be free to do as he or she pleases, either by going out or remaining in. The servant should be encouraged to attend evening classes of an instructive nature, clubs, or to take up a hobby. Of course it would necessitate a small expenditure of money, but it would be beneficial. It would broaden their outlook in life, and make them feel there is more to be found in life than a mere daily routine ; it would not or need not interfere with their work, it would rather prove a stimulus— and it would prove uplifting if their mental as well as their menial qualities had the opportunity of development. Some servants seem to starve from inanition, not because they have not the capacity to enjoy the ideal in life, but because it has not been presented to them. And I have come across many girls who have simply married because they were tired to death of service."

A London general, with thirteen years' experience, who says that she does not regret in the least entering service, for she has always been treated with great kindness, gives the conclusions drawn from her own work :

" I think that if a mistress would only realise that a maid is quite capable of appreciating a good concert or a library, and would arrange for a little time to be allowed to develop a hobby, it would tend to a much happier state of things. I have a good deal to do with young women connected with my own church, and I find they get discontented because they only have time for work. So often I hear it said, ' I can't get a minute ' . . . ' I'd love to go to this lecture or that service, but it is no good to ask, I know I cannot get off.' I hope at the end of this year to be in a position to keep a maid of my own. Since I found out for myself what the life of a maid is like, this is what I shall try to do for her. I should engage a maid who is a Wesleyan. She will always have one, if not two, services of a Sunday. One afternoon and evening a week to visit her friends. In addition I hope to arrange for her to attend one or two of the weeknight services, and arrange for her to be at any social gathering : to give her each day at least one-and-a-half hours to herself, and not to call her from her work to run errands, etc. In return, I shall expect hers to be the service of one who has an ideal and principle guiding her life."

A housekeeper, aged forty, in a household of fifteen, who would " advise those who like housework to enter service, but not those who have been brought up to look upon service as a drudgery, as many do," writes :

" I can only speak as regards large establishments, but think more opportunities should be given for intercourse with others, and a general recreation room provided, and if those in domestic service have any musical knowledge they should be allowed to indulge in it sometimes, and meet one another on the same level as in their own homes, or as our employers do in their own drawing-rooms. There is too much restriction as to every one keeping in their own part of the house. If their work is done well, no harm will come of allowing servants to mix more together and not be always strangers as they often are in a house."

A parlourmaid in a household of seven says she has never put in a year's service, " she could not endure it so long."

Another writes :

" I think that domestic service is cruel to those who have any ambition for business or whatever it might be. For poor people— very poor—it seems the one great thing to have your lodging, washing and bed, practically free. It is much too monotonous to endure day after day without being able either to have friends perhaps to see you, or being able to go and see them ; naturally one loses all interest in life, and it is not worth living."

A very intelligent cook, of over twenty years' standing, says :

" I think every servant should have one evening a week ; there are hundreds never have any chance of amusement, only being allowed a few hours in the afternoons ; in most cases a girl's life is crushed directly she enters service. . . . I think that is why so many mothers keep their girls from it ; they have either experienced it themselves, or see what their relations and friends have to contend with."

"A good cook and an abstainer," wages £30 to £35, who has a few hours off one afternoon in the week, but has late dinners on Sundays, says :

" I am sorry to say I have no other trade I could do; I should be only too pleased to say good-bye to domestic service. We can only describe it as prison without committing crime. . . . No, if a girl has brains, by all means let her make use of them ; the less brains she has in service, the more she can stand the insults from her superiors, so unless she is naturally dull, put her to something more interesting. . . . Every trade has its compulsory hours, but the poor servant is left entirely to the mistress to treat her as she feels, sometimes not very kindly. Why not shorten her hours, or make the wages hourly, but it must and should be compulsory. Why should not we have time for other things besides work ? They should be compelled to let us out once on the Sabbath, and long enough to go a distance. . . . Service in its present state is serious, and if something is not done soon I am afraid it will be the lower class, not the refined girl of years ago that tries service. Ladies will see the difference. They are themselves entirely to blame, we that have had good training always respect our betters when we meet them.

" I have often wished I could have learned shorthand and type-writing, also dressmaking and millinery, as I think these occupations would have helped one to pass off the monotony of domestic service. . . . Service would be better if domestics were given a little more time in which to do as they liked, not to feel tied to answer bells or watch over the cooking, or the other odds and ends that take so much time. If they were to have a time each day away from these things, or to be allowed to have visitors more often, it would lessen the monotony of service a good deal. . . . I think most girls in service would agree with me that we ought to be allowed a little more time for outdoor exercise, as time and work begin to drag heavily when one does not go out for a week, perhaps, when it is your Sunday in. I have heard girls in offices grumbling about having to sit writing all day. Do not domestics get just as tired of their work ? The other girls have at least their free evening to look forward to."

A West-end cook, earning £28, a collar-machinist until she was eighteen ; contented except for lack of free time writes :

" Since I came to service I have had to give up all my church work and musical education. A girl in a shop or factory can take up any social work and also improve her education."

These are fairly good examples ; some replies were

much more strongly worded than those quoted ; some
were less so, but their repetition was very general. It is
worth while to emphasise the desire for outside interests,
whether this be for the night school, or the cinema, or church
and social work, or the conversation of the milkman ;
because well-directed it can do much good, ill-directed
or suppressed it can do much serious harm to the two
human beings, maid and mistress, who are brought
together by the relationship of service.

One solution of the desire to make service less monotonous
is, of course, to interest people more in their work. This
takes form in the desire, only occasionally expressed among
the workers, for better means of training young girls. It is
more often voiced by older servants, lamenting the degen-
eracy of the modern maid. This familiar complaint may
be illustrated by the case of a prosperous children's nurse
who on her husband's death entered service after varied
experiences.

" I would recommend service for any young girl. I myself think
the fault is as much the maids' as the mistresses'. The only way
is to get the girls thoroughly trained, and let them choose a branch of
domestic service congenial to them, then work and domestic service
would be pleasant ; I do not have any outside pleasures, but am
exceedingly fond of the four children of whom I am in charge, and
am devoted to them, and do all in my power to bring them up well.
Many mistresses take a kindly interest in their maids, and are very
kind and good, others again treat their maids as though they had
neither sense nor feeling, and do not allow them to know or understand, and some of the maids are much superior to the women they
have to serve."

A middle-aged parlourmaid is critical ; she has been
in service since fourteen, wages £28 ; no definite hours
out or off duty :—

" I think that the servants in these days do not take enough
interest in their work, but only think of dressing up and going out.
I think if they had more interest in their work they would be happier.
I think that maids that are very much tied should have some free
time to themselves, such as parlourmaids and maids that wait on
invalids. But I certainly think that they are far better off in service
than anything else."

Clearly interest in work is an extremely important
remedy, for if you are so absorbed you are less dependent
on outside interests, in whatever walk of life you may

be—though this is sometimes a doubtful advantage. More sensible house construction and the use of labour-saving devices at home, with possibly some form of co-operative housekeeping, ought in the future to shorten the hours spent by servants in mere drudgery, and to leave more scope for skilled work. But these things will not, *per se*, solve the servant problem.

Many mistresses already try to secure reasonable interests for their maids, and of the seven hundred who replied to the Council's enquiry some gave interesting examples. One of these is quoted at length :—

" I have kept house since my marriage in 1868, and have had many good servants and a few bad ones, though, of course, none are perfect. We began with two maids, and for many years have kept ten or eleven (men and women) and I am very grateful for good service. My present staff have been with me from 21 to 6 years, and except to marry few leave under 10 years or so. But I know this has been good fortune, depending partly on my only accepting *personal* characters—never once going to a registry office—and when a servant is reliable leaving details of time and responsibility in their hands, and trying not to be fidgety. 1 have never allowed any definite hours or days free as a right, but would like them all to go out oftener than they do, and of course approve of them going to church, and to see their friends, who are also welcome to see them, and have tea on Sundays and other days if work allows. Their discretion is good as a rule. Their bedrooms are comfortable, and they see to making them pretty. I approve of pets, and we have now (in London) a dog, a pet cat, and several birds in the servants' quarters. 1 like them to have some artistic interests, drawing, photography and singing."

Others, not a large number, wrote that they give opportunities, which are used, for their maids to go to continuation classes, or to clubs for recreation ; several living in the country with large grounds let the maids have gardens of their own ; a number say that they provide books. With regard to this the scornful comment of one critical servant may be quoted, that the maids only get the " books they have done with, and that they used to read them when they were children."

Attempts from " above " to provide or to share interests are always liable to failure and need discrimination ; but they also need to be tried. You cannot prescribe hobbies for servants any more than for other people, but a sympathetic and imaginative mistress can both suggest them and make them possible.

A special responsibility falls on the mistress with regard to young maids, who are keenly aware that " they are only young once," and who did not in most cases take to the trivial round of household work from a sense of vocation ; while their occupation, though it may in itself be more varied and pleasant than factory work, and probably much less arduous than that of their mothers at home, yet does not give the opportunity for expansion in the evenings and on Sundays, nor the feeling of ownership which lightens drudgery. The life of most modern town children is one constant round of small interests. Those of the classes from which domestic servants are principally drawn, are as a whole surrounded with far more small excitements between the ages of twelve and fourteen than are their richer contemporaries who are being brought up at High Schools or boarding schools. They have short and fairly easy periods of work at school, where for five hours five days a week they are introduced without any strenuous mental effort to the rudiments of many subjects. They may have to give a good deal of help at home out of school, but the majority of mothers shrink from giving their little girls much housework unless forced to do so. In any case they are constantly brought into contact with the real things of life at close quarters, while an abundant variety of guilds, Sunday schools and Bands of Hope offer themselves for their free time. They may possibly suffer from too many interests before going to service ; this will not make it easier for them to accept the severe limitations which service generally imposes on the young beginner. The country girl feels the change much less in this way, but even she must be removed from the human interests of home. Every one who has young friends among these fourteen, fifteen, and sixteen-year-old girls knows how wonderfully silly are the interests that they often may develop, equally at home or in service, when scope is allowed for them. Even so, it is better for them to have some outlets apart from work, and mistresses or older servants should be ready to help make these possible. It is more wholesome for the young person to concentrate her energies even on crocheting impossible mats than on absorbing penny dreadfuls.

Not all girls by any means want intellectual interests either at fifteen or twenty-five, but an increasing number appear to do so. Could not the Workers' Educational Association do something for maids past the stage of continuation classes ? They would find thoughtful material among such members. And could not the older maids who cannot be satisfied with hobbies or intellectual interests be given opportunities of some outside work for other people, preferably for young people or children ? Older women in service, especially those who do not marry, or who marry late, are often obviously stunted for want of something on which to lavish their affections. It is noteworthy that almost all the children's nurses who wrote to the Council were contented, however hard-worked, because they had such an outlet. Such a case has been quoted above in that of the widow who became a nurse. Another delightful nurse wrote :—

" Of course the cook and the housemaid cannot love their saucepans and furniture as I love my babies."

The form which such outside interest would take must naturally depend on circumstances. One obviously happy and placid cook wrote with great pleasure of work that she had been able to do for the " Personal Service Association " ; the mistress of another wrote that she belonged to a Voluntary Aid Detachment and was very keen about it. There is no reason why the domestic servant should be deprived of unpaid social service if she wishes for and is capable of it.

From the national point of view it is deplorable waste that the very capable material to be found in the upper ranks of domestic service should be cut off, as at present, from the needs of the community as a whole. Equally it is great waste of expensive elementary education and of much voluntary work by friends of working-class children that their abundant if superficial interests should not have more reasonable development than service generally affords. If public opinion would secure this for the young maid, perhaps even her chosen amusements would become less foolish than at present they are apt to be.

c

(iv.) Loss of Caste.—This is the most impalpable of all
the objections to domestic service, and one of the most
cogent, for the democratic state, whatever its theories, has
not risen above caring for class differences, in England or
elsewhere. A colonist who took the trouble recently to
write a long letter to the Women's Industrial Council
denouncing the snobbery of the old country, had to
admit that much the same attitude existed in the Dominion
with regard to domestic service. And the girls and quite
young women, who form the bulk of domestic servants,
are apt to be supersensitive on such points.

Those servants who complained about loss of caste in
their replies to the Council's enquiry denounced the contempt shown to them by their employers and by their
own social equals.

The two things are quite different. The first, when it
exists at all outside the maids' own imagination, comes from
sheer lack of manners on the part of the employer. It is a
relic of the time when servility is said to have been expected
from any persons in receipt of wages ; and many people,
knowing the extreme politeness with which they and their
friends try to treat all maidservants with whom they have
to do, and the entire absence of any contempt for them
in their own minds, can hardly believe that it exists. But
the complaint is so widespread that it must have some
basis. When analysed, it seems to consist partly in definite
rudeness from the master and mistress. This is complained
of most commonly as a fault of the self-made employers,
and accounts for the common opinion among maids that
you should not take a place with " people no better than
yourself," but it also appears among employers of a higher
social class, who have not altered the methods of address
of a hundred years ago. It is essentially a charge of neglect on the human side. " They treat us as machines," this
appears constantly ; " as dogs," occasionally, even " as
reptiles." There was nothing in the forms sent to the
servants which could suggest such replies. On the other
hand maids write appreciatively of the employers who
do not treat them as belonging to the " lower orders,"
but take the trouble to show gratitude for and approval of
work well done.

Below are given extracts from letters, which are very moderate samples of what has been often said. Although a good many of these denunciations may be unreasonable and fanciful, yet they show there may often be real cause for complaint. It must be remembered that the maid whose feelings are hurt is not *supposed* to answer back, nor can she go home to allow her feelings an outlet. Therefore there is the greater call for civility between employer and employed.

The complaint, which appears in the first extract, that ladies treat their servants as machines, might be multiplied indefinitely. The writer, now no longer in service, had been for six years lady's maid in " good families." The comment of the orphan general as to the pleasure of working for people who take the trouble to say " thank you," also appears very often. The others need no further remark.

" Service would be more desirable if gentry would think that their servants were as good as they were—I do not mean to be familiar, but treat them as human beings, not as machines."

A general servant, aged twenty-five, brought up at a large orphanage :—

" I think domestic service on the whole is the best occupation a girl or young woman can have, and I find it so nice to do this work so long as the people are grateful with what is done for them."

A London jobbing cook :—

" I have been in very good houses where one is treated as a human being. The better bred people, the *real* gentlefolk, do treat their employees as flesh and blood, the ' jumped up rich middle classes,' *as cattle*. I have not written too strongly, because I have been through it—I have acted both as mistress and servant—and can always verify my statements."

A nurse, earning £30 a year, writes :—

" I consider there are faults on both side in service. When the mistress is kind and thoughtful many of the maids take advantage, which spoils it for those who come after. I myself have been very fortunate, but in some of the houses I have visited with my charges the men and maidservants are treated as if they had no feelings whatever : anything in the way of food will do for the servants. But how can they do their work if not properly fed ? And the way one hears them spoken to sometimes by the master and mistress makes one's blood boil. There is a certain charm about service, but I can understand why so many girls prefer factories, for one is very tied, which with the younger girls gets very monotonous. I do think one has to swallow a great deal of pride in service : of course I went out late and had been my own mistress for many years. . . . I think it would go a long way towards making servants more contented and happy if people would be a little kinder towards them and not treat them as if they were much lower, for after all we are all God's servants."

A cook earning £28 a year :—

" Some ladies expect servants to be like machinery, and don't treat servants like human beings ; others treat one as a friend. My chief complaints are that ladies do not study the servants as servants study them."

" Despised by our own class."—This is in many cases a merely imagined grievance. Almost all the large number of mistresses who wrote about this either denied that maids were despised by any one, or else replied virtually, " *honi soit qui mal y pense.*" ;—maids were well quit of the company of any people, young men or others, who could despise so honourable a calling. From all parts of the British Isles they wrote that maids were not looked down upon by any reasonable people in their neighbourhood, nor were they thought to be in any way unfitted by service for a working man's home, but rather the contrary, especially in the country.

This is almost the only point on which the replies of mistresses and maids were definitely opposed. The maids ought to be the more reliable when they describe the caste difficulties that they actually experience, however unreasonable these may be. The young man who wrote to a paper to say that he knew fellows who would introduce shopgirl sisters to their friends, but never those in service, seems unfortunately to represent a definite type. Below is a heterogeneous collection of opinions on both sides.

A cook in a small household, with twenty-two years' experience :

" I think they might raise the standard of domestic servants ; I think they are looked down upon more than a shop girl and factory girl I was at the Church Social one evening—a lady asked me if I had spoken to the minister during the evening, so I said, ' No, but I live with them.' At once she turned her back on me and never spoke again when she found out I was a servant. We were both old members. Why should they make that difference ? I have seen such a lot of that kind of thing—the difference they make between shop girls and servants : some of the servants out-beat the others in manners and ways."

A cook in London, aged thirty-one :

" I consider servants are a despised race. Not by the ladies, but by girls of their own class who are in business . . . . Of course there are some very good places ; this is one, our lady is not a bit haughty and is really very kind and considerate. I have nothing to complain of here, but I have known ladies who look upon servants as if they were machines. Ill or well, they are expected to do their work, and oftentimes it is not a fair amount . . . . I do not consider work (menial) the least bit degrading, but what I do detest is the scornful phrase ' only a servant ' one constantly hears. When I go to a seaside place and board where there are a number of business girls, I never enlighten them as to how I earn my living. . . . . Of course there are exceptions. I have two very dear friends (of years standing), who are school teachers and several others who are in shops. They are, of course, made of the right stuff, and if I ever say ' servant ' to them they invariably say—' It is not what you do, it is what you are.' "

A cook, aged thirty-two :

" I think service is not at all a desirable post in these days. I often wish some other opening would come my way, as servants are always looked upon as inferior people. I am sure there are a number more good girls working hard in service, than a number of those shop girls whom most ladies sympathise with, and come home telling their maids about them, but don't look at home at all."

A parlourmaid, aged twenty-five :—

" No, I would not advise a girl to enter service, we are made to feel our position too keenly, and we are generally ignored by business and other girls."

A lady's maid, aged thirty-five, in a household of eight :—

" Once a servant, you are treated as belonging to quite an inferior race to all other workers; it is as if the lowest point had been reached."

A cook-housekeeper :—

" I find that although servants must from the very nature of their occupation be of good character, they are not treated with the respect from their employers and others that business women are. This, I think, is a great injustice, and prejudices many a girl against service. It is impossible to go into detail in so short a space, but I think this is one of the chief objections to service."

A house-parlourmaid, aged twenty-eight. She was a

waistcoat-maker till she was nineteen, but is on the whole glad to have left this trade :—

"We are three here, and could not wish for more respectable girls, but still people turn their back on you when you say you are a servant."

An employer writes :—

"The advantages of domestic service as compared with other occupations largely counterbalance any disadvantages. I have kept house for forty years, keeping four indoor female servants; I have for twenty years lived in factory towns, and as head of a large branch of G.F.S. in one town and president of a branch of 300 members of Y.W.C.A. here—all domestic servants—I have some experience. I have found that many factory girls, after two or three years in a factory, leave for service and tell me they are better in health, more comfortably lodged, better fed and have more money as domestic servants. They nearly all have a 'half day out' from 3 till 10 p.m. (We have opened a rest room for them because they are 'out so much.') "

Another employer writes :—

"All my servants who have married, after being with me many years, have married tradesmen in good positions —some with property. Many servants in large establishments marry butlers, stewards, chauffeurs—I speak from personal knowledge—others, general servants, etc., marry tradespeople. I find that good men prefer the domestic servant who can cook and make them comfortable to the shop-girl. I once persuaded a young dressmaker to go to service and found her a place. She took all her sisters from shop and factory, and got them places; they are all well married. . . . I have had a great deal to do with servants—getting them places, hearing their grievances, which I have found very few— as a rule they are contented and happy. They have no anxiety for daily bread, never need be out of place long, are valued in the home. I do not think servants are looked down upon except, perhaps, by silly factory girls, and when they try service they alter their opinion."

A parlourmaid, aged thirty-eight :—

"I think service is the best thing for girls. I find if a girl does her work and duty she is well done by. No doubt there are some bad places; I myself have had two or three, but I have left at the end of a month when I have found how impossible it has been, and that is what I advise any girl to do. The only thing I complain of is the way middle-class people look down upon us; people no better, and often not so well brought up as a good servant, pass remarks like this—' Oh, she is only a servant.' Then they do not want to know us, but I wish people who look down upon servants to understand that no one is so well off as a good servant."

A nurse of twenty-six, personally very content in a household of six :—

" I think it's a great pity that domestic servants are thought so little of, when one knows well-educated girls in service who go because it is a good home, good money and very little expenditure to oneself. Take, for instance, a girl who has been trained at a college for children's nurses, she is treated well in a house and the lady considers her in every way, but directly it is known that she is in service, people say, ' It's best not to know her—she is only a servant."

A suburban parlourmaid, aged forty-four :—

" I would certainly advise service, because I think it does young girls no good to have every evening off to walk the street. . . . I think domestic service would be made better if we were treated with proper respect by both sexes."

A chambermaid in London :—

" The greatest trouble with service is having to wear a cap and apron. Shop girls and business girls look down upon servants for that reason. Otherwise servants are much better off in every sense of the word."

A parlourmaid of twenty-four :—

" The stigma of social inferiority is the drawback. A girl in service is ignored by people in her own social scale, merely because she is a servant."

A cook-housekeeper of thirty-eight, earning £50 a year, writes : "It was not my wish to go into service, but I had no training for anything else." In spite of this she would on the whole advise a young friend to go into service :—

" I think the greatest reason for the discontent among servants is that a servant has no social status whatever. She is always spoken of slightingly and with contempt. She is absolutely nothing and nobody."

It is very difficult to analyse the cause of the " social stigma." Clearly it does exist, but by no means universally. In the country, as many mistresses point out when describing their former maids' marriages, the servants often represent the " aristocracy of the village." In many towns, especially the small towns, the girl who goes into service does not lose caste, partly because there are so few alternative occupations for her. It is chiefly in the suburbs of large towns, and in the industrial districts that the caste difficulty crops up. It does not therefore result from the cleavage between the " soft-handed " and the " hard-handed " occupations. It is due partly—as a good many of the better maids point out—to the lack of self-respect shown by many maids themselves, and partly to the absence of formal training, and the frequent indifference to character which is expressed in the saying that " anyone can be a servant." The artisan and small shop-keeper and farmer whose class, forty years ago, supplied a large proportion of servants, are now able to find more attractive occupation for their daughters elsewhere ; while the greatly increased demand for maids and the spread of elementary education has made it possible for some very poor—even feeble-minded—girls to enter service. The knowledge of this keeps many girls away from service, though the advent of lady servants is doing something, if not yet very much, to raise the status again.

The " social stigma " is in theory an entirely unnecessary stumbling-block to service. It cannot, however, be moved by loftily ignoring it, for " working girls " choose their occupation in life at the age at which girls of any class in life are apt to care most about what " people," namely their own equals, think. The remedy lies partly in fostering public opinion. Juvenile Advisory Committees, backed by the clubs and other social forces that they represent, can be of use here, as they are already trying to be, and anything which can inculcate wholesome views about the dignity of labour in the girls' own class will be of use. There are some signs that the pendulum is already beginning to swing back in favour of service.

But the status of the servant will be raised much more effectively by improvement from within, by better methods of training, by establishing a standard of efficiency for the servant in the middle class house ; still more by recognising the servants' right to a definite time to themselves. The discussions on the National Insurance Act did much to waken the outside world to the requirements of servants as a body, and the Domestic Servants' Insurance Society is the first large organisation which has brought together members of every section of English servants. Perhaps the lady's maid was right when she claimed that the whole social status of servants was being raised when a Duchess held a large reception of servants in connection with the National Insurance Act. This point of view might not satisfy the ardent democrat, but social prejudices can be attacked by different methods. It was partly for this reason, though of course from worthier motives too, that various suggestions were made that the clergy should call upon, or at least recognise the existence of, domestic servants in their parishes. It is worth while for sensible people to make such efforts, for it is very unwholesome for a large and important class of the community either to be despised or to think itself despised.

NOTE.—With regard to the employers' supposed feeling about caste we would quote verbatim the comments of one lady with much experience, though she has misunderstood the perfectly open mind with which the Women's Industrial Council's circular was sent out :

" The scheme seems to imply a fundamental distinction between servants and other people, and I see and feel none. To my thinking any young girl living in one's house is just a young girl : on account of her youth you cannot expect much experience or foresight from her, but you can expect from her an attention to the duties she has undertaken to fulfil ; in return your house ought to become her home, and you ought to take care that she has a pleasant life, sees and makes friends, and gets plenty of open-air exercise, as much as you wish for yourself, and take care to get for yourself. Should you already be old, try and remember your own youth. This is the kind of suggestion I should make for domestic servants, and I should like to see the time when such simple suggestions were no longer necessary. Then domestic service would lose its disagreeables. Its advantages are that in a good house a young girl is properly fed, warmed and housed, has easy conditions and no serious responsibilities during the developing years—fifteen to twenty-five—while she is able to learn a certain amount of method and regularity in daily work, all of which is useful later in life."

Surely if many people had such views and acted upon them, the caste difficulty would soon disappear.

PART TWO

THE INDUSTRIAL ASPECT

WE have tried to analyse fairly some of the psychological problems of domestic service, as they appear to widely distributed employers and maids. We would repeat that this is the fundamental part of the " servant question." We will now, however, consider it from the industrial side, remembering that the two aspects can never really be separated.

In what material ways does domestic service differ from other forms of wage-earning for working-class women and girls ? Its indefiniteness is its essential difference. This is most obvious with regard to wages. It is always harder to fix and to adapt wages in the non-productive than in the productive industries (using these adjectives in the narrowest economic sense), because it is impossible to measure such work directly by total output. But in domestic service the work done cannot be subjected to any comparative test, since it has the character, almost unique in wage-paid industry, of being carried on for use, not for profit, and the settlement of wages remains an individual bargain between employer and employed. Domestic service, again, is the only big industry which is carried on upon the employer's premises, with board and lodging (almost invariably) added to the money wages received. Apart from the Army and Navy, sailors in the merchant service, a diminishing number of agricultural labourers and shop assistants, with a few " living-in " apprentices, domestic servants are now the only representatives of an old system. Their real wages are, admittedly, quite different from the nominal wages which are supplemented by a very indefinite provision of board and lodging, washing and holidays, opportunities for rest, and perhaps of uniform. How far does this unique relationship work out satisfactorily for employer and employed ? Normally, when discussing and assessing the real wages of an industry, the opportunities of advancement and of providing for old age are considered. Are these prospects better or worse in service than in factory, shop, and office work ?

The organisation of all industries is becoming more and more important to society as a whole. What reasonable provision is made in service for the entry of beginners and for their training ? Do standards of efficiency exist for the employers and employed in the totally different branches of service ? Is the existing method by which labour circulates satisfactory ? Is there a growing demand for a new type of servant (and employer) ?

Until recent years the legislator, the inspector and the economist had (for better or worse) left domestic service severely alone, as a thing apart from the industrial world. "If only they had continued to do so," cry uncounted mistresses and maids. But you cannot isolate industrial problems, and when an important industry is, clearly, not keeping up its numbers or developing in efficiency in proportion to increased demand, it is only commonsense to analyse the causes and consider remedies.

These are some of the questions, constantly and inevitably raised in discussions on domestic service. Some light, will, we hope, be thrown on them in the next two divisions.

I—REAL WAGES

(i.) ACCOMMODATION.—The creature comforts obtainable in domestic service are its great recommendation in the eyes of many parents and contented women. "I shall always say that if a girl has her living to get she cannot do better than go into private service, where you have good food and a good bed to lie on." So wrote a general servant of thirty-one who left home "quite of her own accord" when she was eleven, and had had only four places in that time. Many would agree with this. But even in good private service there are complaints of the accommodation provided for servants. It is noteworthy that a larger proportion of mistresses than of servants wrote of this. People who have been brought up in poor houses must, under present housing conditions, become inured to un-

necessary discomforts. But it is no adequate defence of
bad accommodation for servants to say, as is sometimes
said, that in any case it is much better than they would
get in their own homes.

Complaints concern chiefly :—

1. Basement kitchens, their lack of air, sun, and cheer-
   fulness.
2. Insanitary conditions, as to papering, etc., of kitchens.
3. Sleeping accommodation ; overcrowding, and basement bedrooms.[1]

The problem of accommodation is, like so many building
problems, largely a bequest from the past. Employers as
well as servants suffer from the amazing domestic architecture of two and three generations ago. It is hard to see
how to improve these basement rooms, except to secure that
those who live in them have frequent and regular access to
sun and fresh air, and have wholesome sleeping apartments.
With regard to these, new buildings, and especially flats,
are often as defective in bedroom accommodation as
the Victorian and pre-Victorian houses. A number of
mistresses and of servants pointed this out with
emphasis. The servants' room in these is apt to be very
ill-ventilated, and very small. Employers, and certainly
builders, do not appear to realise the change in the desire
for fresh air (both by day and night) that is coming over all
classes in the present generation. Possibly those were
right who said that we should never get real structural
improvement until we have women architects. It might
be more true to say that improvement depends on whether
women will take the trouble to think out what they want,
and produce an educated demand upon their architects.[2]

[1] See Appendix iv.
[2] We insert the comment of an experienced architect. "For one
house properly designed by an architect, at least fifty are built by the
speculative builder, cheapness being the first consideration. 'Ordinary
Domestic Architecture,' means, therefore, the speculative builders'
'architecture.' His custom is to place the servants' bedroom in the
roof, which in August is the hottest room in the house and in January
the coldest. Any alteration in this arrangement would increase the cost
of building and consequently does not obtain. I fear that *sometimes* the
space with no ventilation, marked in the plan passed by the authorities
as a 'boxroom,' has been used as a servant's bedroom. It is the
lodging-house servant that is most frequently sinned against."

Until the old houses have ceased to exist, there cannot be great structural improvements ; but reasonable thoughtfulness can secure cheerful surroundings. Only five servants out of the six hundred who sent in replies to the Council acknowledged to sharing a bed with a fellow servant, and most of them, as well as the mistresses, replied to the question with a surprise that showed that this custom is almost extinct. A few mistresses justly pointed out that some young girls prefer to share a bed at first. All agreed that a maid should have a right to a bed to herself. Instances of simple forms of consideration are given by some good mistresses from their own practice ; such as the supply of screens, or of cubicles when rooms must be shared, of armchairs in the kitchen or the servants' sitting room, and the provision of reasonable opportunities for baths. (A number of maids express a desire, quite unprompted, for the occasional use of the bath-rooms.) Everyone will feel some sympathy with the maid who wrote that all she had to do with a bathroom was to wash four dogs in it weekly ! Quotations in the next section illustrate the maids' point of view. But mistresses expressed themselves more strongly than maids on the whole of this question of accommodation. What remedies are possible beyond those which individual consideration can secure ? Inspection of servants' premises has often been suggested ; twenty per cent. among the mistresses who replied were in favour of this : the rest metaphorically held up their hands in horror, though a very few were prepared for some new official agency to inspect rooms offered to very young servants, as is frequently done on behalf of the Metropolitan Association for Befriending Young Servants, and of Boards of Guardians responsible for poor-law children. Probably it would be fair, in the state of public opinion, to inspect servants' rooms in hotels and in lodging-houses already registered. A number of successful mistresses who " have never had any trouble " with servants say they always show or offer to show new servants their bedrooms before engaging them, or to let another servant show them over the maids' part of the house. Several of these mistresses, it may be noted, say that this offer is constantly refused.

(ii.) Food.—There were not many complaints on this

head.　Such as were made—and these are typical—came
from

(a) Very small households, where the "general" was
underfed owing to poverty of employers ;
(b) Some hotels ;
(c) Large households where the mistress does not supervise what goes on below stairs. The cook will not
always trouble to prepare proper meals for the
other servants, and good food does not penetrate
beyond the housekeeper's room, or only reaches
the servants' hall after 10 p.m.

There was probably truth in the view of the housekeeper who said that it was much harder to provide for
the servants' hall than for the dining-room, for the occupants
of the former were much more fastidious ; but the question
of meals is a point for the head of the household to look
into, especially with young servants.

These quotations are gathered from the replies of different
classes of servants who answered the Council's enquiry.

" I am afraid that inspection is more than necessary, accommodation being one of the greatest evils, some of the kitchens being very
detrimental to our health ; that can be easily remedied. Sanitary
inspectors should give the poor people a rest and visit some of the
large houses : if they were shown our apartments there would be a
good many empty kitchens. I think it is a general rule to have a
bed each."

A cook-general, twenty-three years in service :—

" I have had a wide experience of domestic service, having lived
in large houses, and know too well the life, on account of bad living
(food), unhealthy surroundings, over-work and no rest, no out-door
outings (very limited). I have had to take small places at great
sacrifices on account of being run down ; I am now more comfortable, but it's a great sacrifice after years of hard work to be a cook-
general, and I owe it to the conditions of service."

A London general at £20 a year, aged thirty-nine ;
on the whole contented with her lot :—

" Provided she liked housework and was very willing, I would
advise a girl to enter service, but I think a reform greatly needed is,
that a maid should be *shown* her *bedroom* and *kitchen* before deciding
to accept the situation."

A London cook at £30 a year.   Eight years in service :—

" Not on any account should a girl go to service under the present conditions.

" The improvements wanted are more consideration shown by employers, better food and outings, a stated time for meals, and not expected to do men's work, as taking up and laying down carpets, beds, etc., which have been the ruin of many a poor girl, and filling up the hospitals with cases which need not have been. Private houses should come under Government, and sanitary inspectors should visit these houses the same as the poorer ones, as I know of several where the maids sleep in the basement, where there is no means of fresh air, and only the smell of cooking and drains. Is it any wonder, then, that there are so many delicate and pale-faced girls to be met always ? It is quite time this was looked into.

This cook in a small suburban household wrote a long letter, and had had experience of many " bad " places :—

" I was trained by a lady who took me when quite young after my mother's death ; was with this lady for some years. I am now forty-seven years of age, and up to the last, I might say, ten years, got on fairly well, had good wages, and was with fairly nice people. If I found a place did not suit, would leave and get something better, but of late have had great difficulty in finding anything good ; some of the bedrooms have been anything but what they should have been, also the food, and that very scarce. I went to another place, and *never* saw such a kitchen. I do not know where the sanitary inspectors are ; the stench was poisonous. Was out of that place the next day.

" If employers would only treat their servants as if they were human beings, feed them better, and know how to speak, and show a little kindness and consideration, and trusted them more I am quite sure there would not be so much sin going on at the present day. Then people are saying there are no good servants. Do they know how to keep them ? Do they do their duty to them when they get them into the house ? But they expect the servant to do hers, and even more than her duty. Let them put it to themselves. How would *they* like food of a cheap and inferior kind got for them ? No place for rest during the day for five minutes, to keep on day in, day out ; *never* to go out unless you have leave, not a creature to come and see them, but grind on and on ? "

A Surrey cook, aged forty-eight, wages £24, wrote with great moderation and with personal contentment :—

" Concerning the kitchens and bedrooms. I am sure the Sanitary Inspectors ought to visit the houses of the rich as well as the poor ; they would be surprised at the state of the servants' apartments. The kitchens, of course, are not seen by visitors to the house, so it does not matter. If they happen to be situated in the front of the house, shrubs are grown to hide them, no matter how dark it makes it, or how much fresh air is thus shut out, and where is it more necessary for fresh air than where food is being constantly cooked ? The smells must not go upstairs or there is soon a fuss."

A cook, twenty years in service, £26 a year :—

"I have been where four or five servants had to sleep in one room. Is that healthy ?"

A cook in a large household, aged forty-six, wages £36, wrote very reasonably :—

"Personally I've had very comfortable places, and sometimes very hard ones with late hours . . . but I should like to say with regard to servants who live in flats I think it is dreadful, they never think about any comfort for them and even send some of them to sleep in the roof at the top of the mansions, also all servants should be provided with a bath-room or a bath and towels. . . . I'm at present in a very comfortable place and a kind mistress."

Housemaid waitress in a London hotel with fifteen servants, £18 a year, aged twenty-nine :—

"They should give better bedrooms for girls, not where you have to sleep in a basement and perhaps four or five girls sleeping in one room. Of course some places are good, and some are not. But every place should provide better sleeping accommodation. That is why so many girls get ill because they do not get proper ventilation."

Chambermaid of thirty-three, in a set of flats, earns £18, and has to buy uniform and spend four or five shillings a week on food ; gets very small tips. Went there for the sake of freedom and fixed time off, but hates it :—

"It is better in some ways than the private houses with hours from 6.30 to 10 or 11 p.m. with hardly a break. Our food is bread and butter for breakfast, tea and supper all the year round, and our dinners are very poor indeed, so we have to pay out something to keep up our strength, and the work is very heavy. I have to attend to four flats, with thirteen rooms and two bathrooms, nine grates. . . . Some of the bedrooms are very bad for the girls, which they are in most big places. I know of five and six girls sleeping in one room with hardly any ventilation, and generally in the basement."

A thoughtful Scotch lady's maid :—

"I would advocate for the entire abolition of underground kitchens and servants' sitting-rooms, etc., they are an abomination to civilization, and the ruin of many girls' health."

(iii.) HOURS OF WORK AND TIME OUT.—A servant is normally liable to be called on at any moment between rising and going to bed ; that is, she is theoretically on duty from 6.30 a.m. to 10 p.m. or later. Put in this way, the hours of work are indeed preposterous. Except in certain very hard situations, or at times of special pressure, the work is emphatically not incessant throughout these fifteen and a half hours. Many servants have two or three hours of leisure apart from mealtimes if the spare minutes scattered throughout the day are reckoned together. More servants could have such free time if they got through their work more quickly or if they chose to plan out their own work, and arrange a system of give and take with fellow-servants. Here comes in the need both for training in good methods of work, and for the grouping of maids who " get on well together." The work is, of course, done at much less high pressure generally than is that of work-shops ; some zealous maids with real zest for their work do not complain at all about the length of time which they spend upon it, and some would always be resigned to " muddle along " throughout the day, as their mothers very possibly did at home. But to many temperaments this sort of long-drawn detailed work is much more fatiguing than is harder work for a shorter time, as the " business " woman in the professional classes will often admit when she comes to live at home and manage a household and family.

What leisure hours does a maid have every week ? All the servants consulted were asked this. Their replies varied considerably according to their special occupation. Several children's nurses said that they had no time off at all and did not want it, as they liked so much being with their little charges ; a number of parlourmaids said they had no time at all for themselves in the house, and out of doors only fortnightly Sunday evenings with a weekly afternoon ending in time for a late dinner, while various country servants said that they had a whole day free every month instead of a weekly holiday. The majority had an outing from three, four, five, or six p.m. to seven, eight, nine, ten p.m., that is, from three to seven hours on one weekday ; and the same time on alternate Sundays, with probably time for Church on the other Sunday morn-ing. There are many variations on this, however. Some-

D

times the free Sunday afternoon comes only once in three weeks ; sometimes not at all in the case of cooks and parlourmaids in households where there is much Sunday entertaining. (About this there were many lamentations.)

With regard to time that they have to themselves indoors, the majority, especially parlourmaids, said that they had none on weekdays ; if not actually at work, they were always liable to be summoned. About a quarter said that they had one hour a day free.

The desire either for limitation of hours of work or for some regular time off daily seems to be spreading very widely, partly inspired by the example of the hospital nurse, partly stimulated by the Shop Hours Act, which has brought the possibilities of Government regulation of working hours in a visible form before all.

We give a large number of extracts from the replies that reached us, both favourable and unfavourable to present conditions. These replies are typical of very many to the same effect. Some of them sound very bitter, but a considerable variety of opinions have been deliberately quoted to illustrate the striking unanimity on the subject among maids of different classes. It is one of the few points in which the many grades embraced in domestic service unite. The mistresses circularised were also consulted on the point. Most of them agreed on the desirability of leisure, but said very truly that it was very difficult to make hard and fast rules on this as on other points of domestic service ; that service was based on the idea that the maid became part of her employer's family, and like other feminine members of a family, she must expect to share its life and needs. They insisted that very often it was the servants' own fault if they did not get free time, either because they did not know their work, or because they would not take turns with each other over it. But the careful employers agreed that by skilful management—perhaps by drawing up a domestic time-table—some leisure ought to be secured to each of their household every day, and that all but very young servants should be allowed to settle among themselves as to going out beyond the definitely agreed times, without asking leave on every occasion. But the need for loyalty reappears here. Both mistresses and maids quote

instances of places where the maids used to have time off
and go out freely, but this privilege had been withdrawn,
because it was made an excuse for neglecting work.
The following are extracts from some employers' statements.

The first is from a lady doctor :

" My housemaid has twenty-three hours a week off duty ; so
has my maid ; the cook has eighteen hours off."

" Mine have two or three hours a day free, and in the evening play
halma, old maid, etc."

" Why should servants not have definite hours off duty ? In
India they go home from 12—2 and after 9 p.m."

" It is certainly desirable that servants should have definite
hours off duty, but it is hardly possible in a small house where there
are children."

" It is impossible to fix these hours definitely, but there is no
difficulty in securing them in a well-ordered house."

Both the Girls' Friendly Society Central Registry and
the Guild of Dames of the Household endeavour to secure
certain hours off duty. The latter makes it a condition
of engagement that two hours' freedom should be promised
daily.

The following quotations are taken from a variety of
statements made by servants :—

" I am a cook and have been in service twenty years, and feel
sure I could make a few suggestions. I am in a hard place now.
I rise early and am at work all day long. First thing in the morning
every day I have to light four or five fires and clean the steps before
breakfast, besides cleaning the breakfast-room, cooking breakfast,
cleaning boots, fetching up hot water and tea to those upstairs. I
get out but for a few hours once a week.

" I think servants' hours of labour much too long, and I wish
with all my heart the Factory Act limiting the hours of labour could
be applied to domestic service. Good sorts of people, I feel sure,
would not mind."

A nurse from Lincolnshire, earning £18 :—

" Certainly I should advise any young friend to enter service.
My own experience has been anything but unhappy ! And I think,
as a rule, service is far better for girls than shop or factory work.

" I think all girls should be allowed a certain time off—say, a
whole day once a month, or one night : I do not think two or three
evenings a week till nine or ten at night do a girl much good, unless
they have home or friends near, where they can go, or have some one

to go about with ; let them get a good walk, or ride, every day, if possible, and a free *day* every four weeks, and as much time on Sunday as can be fairly arranged ; most girls would, I think, be satisfied."

A parlourmaid, began work at thirteen, now earning £22 : Time out given as 3.30–7 on one weekday, with two hours on alternate Sundays and no free time in the house :—

" I do not recommend service. Young people now have better openings for them, and long service is not appreciated as of earlier years. A regular time is wanted for on duty and off duty, so that each one might have a little time to call their own ; also if employers could understand that servants are human creatures and not mere machines."

A general of twenty-five, eleven years in service :—

" I think we ought to be allowed a certain time off duty every day, for where I am I do not even have time to do my own mending ; there is only me kept ; I have all the work of the house to do, which amounts to rather a lot for £16 a year."

" For any girl who can get into a *good* place to start, I think service as happy a life as any—if the mistress is kind, and takes any interest in her maids, but so often servants do not get sufficient out-door exercise.   I think one of the chief drawbacks to service is that one feels so tied always, and scarcely ever free.   Few ladies realise that servants often need to be as much in the fresh air as themselves, and also that recreation is as much needed by servants as any other class of workers."

A nurse earning £30 in family where eleven servants were kept :—

" It was my parents' wish that I should go to service, and as a child I looked forward to the time when I should serve in a lady's house.   I certainly do advise young girls to go into service : I believe it to be the most respectable employment for girls and women.   I believe if girls were allowed about one or two hours' entire freedom from duty every day either in the house or out, it would make a great difference."

A daily servant, at 5s. a week :

" No, I would not advise a friend to go to service, because you never know when you are finished, and if you work two or more hours' overtime, you are not paid any extra money as you are in a factory.   I think a bill ought to be passed compelling mistresses to give their maids so much time each week, or each day when convenient, so that if the maid has any shopping to do, or any errands to perform it can be done.   It is usually bedtime when I am finished work.   Sometimes I get half an hour in the evening, and about three hours on Sunday."

Lady's maid in large household ; wages £34, dressmaking till twenty-two ; free time, an occasional hour during the week when convenient, 3–7 and 3–10 alternate Sundays :—

" For girls without homes or friends service is, perhaps, best, but I have tried both business and service, and in the latter the food is better and more regular, but there is no give and take. You are completely in the power of the lady, and can be called upon day or night. Until servants are given stated hours for work, and more freedom, like every other worker, girls will not enter service. To me in my particular branch of work, the great need is shorter hours ; the long, weary hours of sitting up, after a day's work is done, is very tiring. For many nights in succession, I do not go to bed till the early hours of the morning, but the day's work is expected just the same, and you are not expected to be tired."

A general earning £18 a year :—

" I think from remarks that I have often heard servants say, it would be a good thing if a mistress would only allow a maid to have an hour each day entirely to herself in her bedroom ; if they would only think how many of us servants get to look on our bedroom as our own little private home.

" I would like to say my first place was in a family of seven servants, but after two years of it I decided to try as a general servant and have never regretted it. 1 had only worked as a field worker in the country before I entered service.

" My mother and father sent us all to service : a family of eleven, they had eight girls, three boys ; all the girls went to service ; three were cooks and myself now ; the others housemaids. They are all married now except one of my sisters and myself. The time one gets to themselves, I think, greatly depends on the maid herself ; if she is methodical in her work and manages it well she could always get a little spare time."

A London house-parlourmaid, about thirty (£24 a year) :—

" Is there no remedy which will do away with such long hours : for instance, the servants who work in lodging houses, hotels and clubs ? I have worked in the latter and, therefore, know, from 6 or 6.30 till 11 or 12 o'clock at night."

A nurse of thirty in a large household, earning £35 a year :—

" I think every girl should have proper time off, also enough time for meals, such as an hour for dinner, half-an-hour for breakfast and tea, and set hour for getting up and leaving off, not to be kept on all hours of the night. Some ladies, I find, expect one to keep on and on, and think no more of a girl for doing it." (She would advise a young friend to go into service " because they nearly always have a decent bed to lie in, and meals at stated times ready to sit down to and money coming in regular.")

A cook-general, aged thirty-one, wages £24 a year. Started at thirteen :—

" I think service is far better for a girl than factory, as we are sure of plenty of work and food and our money is regular. . . . I am very glad something is being done for domestics, as I think the factory girls are studied far more than we are. I think there ought to be laws for us as well as for them. When they have done their day's work they have done, but we have finished when it is time for bed. Why shouldn't domestic servants have a half day once a week ? "

A cook-housekeeper of thirty-one, at £27 a year :—

" I went into service because I was fond of housework and liked the idea of possessing a box of clothes of my own, and because I fear I looked down on the average business girl and thought servants were more refined and ladylike. I knew also that I would be able to keep myself at once, and would cease to be a burden on my parents ; being the eldest of a large family, I was anxious to help them all I could. I have never regretted that I chose service as my occupation."

(She wants " that it should be compulsory for all mistresses to give an afternoon and evening, say from 2.30 or 3 o'clock till 10 p.m. every week or its equivalent in addition to the usual Sunday outing. It is *not* an unreasonable request, and pure selfishness on the part of the mistresses that refuse.")

A stillroom maid in household of nearly twenty :—

". . . The girls here are up at 5 or 5.30, and retire to bed about 11 with only bare time for meals in the kitchen and stillroom. These people . . . are very nice themselves, but I am sure they do not know what goes on below stairs."

A parlourmaid :—

" I went to service because it was the only thing suitable, as I was trained to be a teacher, but voice was not strong enough through the effects of diphtheria.

" Certainly I should *not* advise a friend to go to service :

(1) Because servants are treated as machines and not human beings.

(2) Because servants can never be sure of free time, as so often there are parties to stop it.

" Reforms needed are these :—

(1) Characters of mistresses to be given to servants before entering their employ.

(2) A set time for leaving off work the same as they have in shops and factories.

(3) An outing each week, irrespective of croquet, tennis and other parties which often stop them.

" I cannot write anything for it, but could write sheets against it."

A parlourmaid, aged thirty-five, wages £28 :—

" It is often in the best places in other ways that the outings are the worst."

A trained lady servant, now in Canada :—

" No, I would not advise a friend to enter service if she was able to do anything else. Because generally speaking there is no freedom from work. Creature comforts are generally good, but other things nil. Get legislation for a twelve hours' day. If domestic service could claim the rightful amount of liberty, healthy rooms in which to sleep and work, a feeling of good fellowship between mistress and maid, and social life outside, I could not say enough in praise of it or to recommend it to others. As it is I have been driven out of it by too long hours of work and unhealthy rooms in which to work. The hours have nearly always been from fourteen to sixteen hours on end. . . . As a stenographer in Canada I now have seven and a half hours daily instead of from fourteen to sixteen, and Saturday afternoons and Sundays all day off."

Probably many more mistresses would make opportunities for their servants to take even short walks daily and would urge them to avail themselves of these, if it occurred to them to do so. A generation which talks much about health, should also consider the need, especially for young maids, of adequate hours of sleep, and of some period of rest in the middle of the day. Varicose veins and other troubles, as well as " nerves," come largely from the constant standing that the kitchen girl has to do, and from the running up and down of the between-maid and the hard-worked general during their unlimited hours of work. These are essentially matters for mistresses (and the parents of young maids) to consider, for the girls themselves and older servants are apt to be foolishly inconsiderate about them.

Any discussion such as the above, of the hours of work in domestic service, brings home to us once more the very different conditions and needs of the different classes of servants. But the desire for some definite remission of work is so widespread even among the personally contented, that it deserves reasonable consideration. Remedies are suggested, which fall under four headings. First, that all servants should have a compulsory legal half-holiday, either on the same day of the week, or on days to be settled by mutual agreement. A large number of them get this already, but it is felt by many that such a legal recognition of the servants' rights would do much to raise their industrial status. Why should they be neglected, when legislation is hedging the path of other workpeople at every step ? There would, however, be need for special provision for young servants with regard to this. The reluctance of all good employers to give " evenings out " to the young maids unless they have relations and friends or perhaps a good club within reach, is *not* due to mere selfishness or fussiness.

Secondly, it is urged by a number that in addition to a half-holiday, the hours of work should be definitely limited to a certain number a day. According to some progressive mistresses and some branches of the working women's societies which were consulted these hours should be eight ; according to the programme of the Domestic Workers' Union, ten ; according to the piteous appeal of a former lady servant—safeguarded while in service by a merely nominal guarantee of two hours' leisure per day—twelve.

Thirdly, it is often urged that a definite period of time off—even one hour a day—should be secured to all servants, either by law or by convention, and that their mealtimes should be free from interruption.

And, fourthly, it is proposed by a very modern school, that the problem could be partly, at least, solved by the organisation of (efficient) servants, living at home, or in special hostels, and coming for a few hours a day at so much per hour, to their employer's house. This would not be favoured at present by the majority, either of employers or maids. The daily servant of the present is apt to be the least efficient of her class, and her position offers obvious difficulties with regard to cleanliness and in temptation to small forms of dishonesty, as well as other dangers. These drawbacks are not, however, inherent in the position of the daily servant, and the household problem will probably be materially lightened in the future by the spread of a really good type of daily servant. This is already being done on a small scale on behalf of London flat-dwellers.

Allowing for the present mismanagement of their time by many maids, for the difficulty of standardising free time in domestic service, and for the desirability *cæteris paribus* of leaving these matters to be amicably settled within the household, we feel strongly (1) that all servants should have on an average two hours off duty per day, exclusive of reasonable allowance for mealtimes ; and (2) that all servants should have either at least one weekly half-holiday, besides Sunday, or its equivalent on two afternoons per week. If this can be secured by organised public opinion among servants and their employers, so much the better. If not, it will be essential to resort to legislation. But in service it is much better to avoid the rigidity which legislation must impose.

For one point often mentioned together with the desire for more free time, probably many of the employing class will feel sympathy. This is the need for more opportunities of fresh air, even for short periods. An artisan father who wrote to the Women's Industrial Council a long and interesting account of the vicissitudes which attended the first year spent in service by his daughter, a fifteen-year-old paragon from a London County Council School, mentioned, as one of the few satisfactory things which befell her, that one of her London employers sent all the four or five maids of the household out together for ten minutes before they went to bed. A number of mistresses wrote on this point :—" My servants (country) have a day off a month, and at least a half-hour out every day." " Mine "—in Eaton Square— " can all go out every day." " Mine can go out every afternoon if they like, but they do not choose to do so " (Rochdale). " This is very difficult to manage with one servant." " Mine can go out every day, though at irregular times." " Mine have almost daily walks." " My general servant goes out every day."

The desire for fresh air is genuine in many cases, and is probably new. Below are given a few instances of the servants' views on the subject.

A parlourmaid in a private school, where she is personally very contented :—

" I think it ought to be made possible for every maid in turn to have an hour every day, as is arranged here, so that the maid can go to her room to be at rest, and, if she wants, sew for herself. . . . No conscientious maid puts her work before her mistress. . . .

If it could be arranged, some young girls in service ought to be allowed the same hour for a walk in the open air if they wished it, as so many get anæmic."

A parlourmaid in Staffordshire vicarage, £20. No fixed time out :—

" My mother and father, being sensible people, did not wish me to go anywhere else than to domestic service, neither did I wish it myself, and as I was the eldest of eight children, I was very glad to do something to help at home. I think it is a very good way of earning our living and would advise every young girl to go in for it, in preference to factories, etc., and I think every girl should have a good knowledge of housework, which they cannot possibly have if they have no experience.

" I think it would be a great boon to domestics if they could have a certain length of time off duty every day, such as hospital nurses have ; say half an hour, or even more if possible, exercise in the fresh air every day, and an hour each day for their own needlework."

A nursemaid of eighteen :—

" I think I advise any young girls to go to service. What I think should be done is to secure young girls before they go out to work so that they cannot realise the difference in freedom they obtain in comparison with that of service, as it is generally night freedom. . . . . I, too, think that some girls, especially delicate girls, ought to have outdoor freedom every day, as I know for a truth that some girls would stay in their situations more contentedly if only they had freedom."

A cook from Twickenham, aged twenty-eight :—

" I am pleased to say I am very happy. I've a very kind and considerate mistress. I take turns with the house parlourmaid with the outings, which are every other Sunday and one afternoon a week from 2 to 10 ; then besides that we take in turns of having one the afternoon, the other the evening ; that is how we go on all the week through. I am cook here, and am getting £25. I feel sure that if ladies would only let their maids out a little more often they would be much happier and able to work much better. P.S.—I think myself service is the best for girls, but you must take the rough with the smooth."

A cook-general at £18 a year :—

" There are many things which might be improved ; for instance, one week I am out on Thursday from half-past five till ten, and except for two hours Sunday morning I am not out till the next Thursday : I think something might be done so that we could go out for a little time oftener than that as I get such bad headaches, and if only I could go out for an hour every day I should never have one. Otherwise I think service is the *best place for girls*."

(iv.) MONEY WAGES.—Very few of the servants reached by the enquiry of the Council volunteered remarks about their payment in money. A few of those in small houses said that they wanted less work and more wages ; a few older servants wrote, as if in reply, that " if girls nowadays will stand out for high wages they must expect hard work " ; but it was their " real " not their " monetary " wages that they discussed chiefly. All were asked whether their wages were paid during their holidays. The replies revealed how universal the fortnight's holiday is in the servant's year, the only exceptions being in the case of those who by their own or their employer's fault change their places too often to earn a holiday, or in the case of some young beginners. Quite a large percentage said that they had three or four weeks' holiday in the year ; all but three said that their wages were paid during their holidays. In very few cases, however, were board wages paid, except occasionally when the holidays lasted longer than a fortnight. A few modern servants said that board wages ought to be given during all holidays, because board and lodging were included in the payment for service. This is a question on which it is difficult to be quite logical. In theory, perhaps, board wages should be paid ; in practice, there seems no great demand for their payment during a short holiday. Universal insistence on their payment would be a considerable strain on the small middle-class employer, and would, probably, lead to a curtailment of holidays. The difficulty of financing a holiday comes home most to the poorly paid servant, the beginner, or the inefficient. It is not easy to save up for a holiday and fares, as well as to put money in the savings bank, out of a wage of four or five shillings a week, and in the case of servants with no homes to which to go, a holiday, even among friends who have to be paid, is a difficulty. This is a difficulty which ought to be solved by consideration on the part of the employer.

In the circulars sent out to employers, two incompatible suggestions that sometimes appear in discussions of the servant question were thrown out. The first of these proposed that a minimum wage for servants should be established by law. This the employers, with almost complete unanimity, declared to be quite unnecessary, since wages have risen so greatly without any legal inter-position ; and quite impossible, because the conditions of service vary so much, both in requirements and in remuner-ation.   Even granting that in the establishment of a legal minimum wage provision were made for the learner and the inefficient, how could a rigid rate possibly be adapted to the peculiarities of the individual servant and employer ? How much should you deduct from the legal wage for a housemaid or a cook in return for the installation of vacuum cleaners or gas-cookers of varying types of efficiency ? How much should you add to it because the back stairs were built at an angle of 45°, or the employer's family leave their possessions about the house and always come in late to meals ? It is impossible to assess minimum rates without definite reference to work done, and domestic work cannot be definite.   A few small organisations of married working women and a branch of the Domestic Workers' Union were in favour of a legal minimum wage.   But they gave no reasons for this and no apparent consideration to its practical difficulties.

The second suggestion made was worded as follows : " There is in service no standard of wages asked or offered in relation to a standard of efficiency. . . .   An organisa-tion of servants should be formed, guaranteeing the efficiency of its members, and in return receiving a wage above the minimum."

This might be delightful, said many of the employers, if the guarantee of efficiency were really effective.   But unless the organisation undertook the training and examina-tion of servants—which would of course be possible—this would be difficult.   As a matter of fact, as was pointed out, there is already a local standard of servants' wages, varying in different parts of the country, which has at least theoretical relationship to efficiency.   There are or have been already organisations of trained charwomen, of waitresses, of supply cooks, which do more or less guarantee efficiency in relation to a fixed daily wage.   Some of the organisations of lady servants, such as the Dames of the Household and Norland Nurses, successfully enforce a money minimum below which they will not supply workers.

There are some schools and homes which supply well-trained girls of sixteen and seventeen for first places, and there is scope for more development of this sort in the upper class of domestic service. It opens a field for a good organiser, either among servants if such can be found, or among educated workers.

The employers' replies showed that they did not shrink for selfish motives from the enforcement of a general minimum wage, whether legal or by agreement. They all felt that they already paid highly for their servants and that the minimum wage would not probably be much higher, and might be well compensated by guaranteed efficiency. But they were against any rigid delimitation of rights and duties, partly from sentimental dislike of outsiders intruding into the home, partly from the commonsense objection that a legal rate would be impossible to adjust fairly, and that in the present state of supply and demand it was quite unnecessary from any point of view.

(v.) UNIFORMS.—The cost of uniform must obviously be deducted from the net wages that the servant earns, and it is sometimes said that this is one of the drawbacks to service. We feel clearly that this is one of the imaginary drawbacks. Few working women have the chance of wearing clothes which are both so practical and becoming as the maid's cotton dresses and aprons, and very few servants alluded to uniforms among the points of service which they wished to see improved. The cost of the clothes is to some extent a burden. The business girl indeed often has to spend more on dress than the maidservant needs to do, but the girl in a factory or workshop spends small sums on her working clothes. " If a uniform is needed the mistresses should supply it. A factory worker finds nothing but a pair of scissors, all other tools being found by the firm ; asking girls to find their own uniform is like asking factory workers to find their own machinery ; they cannot afford it," wrote a factory worker with some knowledge of service.

Where a special uniform is prescribed, beyond the conventional black dress and aprons, the employer almost always provides or helps to provide it. Hardships really only occur in the case of quite young maids, and of those

with "faddy" mistresses who require that special patterns
of caps and aprons shall be worn in the house, and, perhaps
occasionally, that bonnets shall be worn at church.   If
these are insisted on help should obviously be given towards
providing them.   A few lamentations about such fastidious-
ness were sent from suburban villas.

One practical suggestion was made by several sensible
maids ; that after a recent custom in some shops,
cotton dresses or white blouses should sometimes at least
be substituted in hot weather for the whole black dress.
Probably the "superior" domestic servant would be the
first to resent this suggestion, but it seems eminently
sensible.   It is only for one generation that the black dress
has been universal for a maid's afternoon and evening
wear.

The briefest discussion of servants' uniforms would not
be complete without some allusion to caps.   Any objection
to the maid's special dress that may be felt, apart from those
described above, centres round caps.   From the utilitarian
point of view they are now generally valueless and there
seems little reason why they should be worn.   There are
maids who say that, owing to their hated headdress, they
cannot put their head out of doors without being called
"skivvy" by passing workmen or errand boys.   The
young person whom we quote below is probably typical of
these.

"The great improvements needed in domestic service are the
abolition of the Insurance Act and the abolition of caps.   A cap has
never made a bad girl good or a good girl better ; I have heard
several girls say that they wouldn't mind going into service if they
hadn't to wear caps.   The dresses they didn't mind, but the caps
were generally referred to as the trademark of modern slavery."

But the dislike of caps is surely the effect, not the cause,
of the supposed loss of caste involved in service as a whole.
The country loves uniforms and badges, and is constantly
inventing fresh forms of these for its younger citizens.
The sick nurse's uniform now only secures respect ; children's
nurses can wear their special dress out of doors with complete content ; the Dames of the Household have their
own uniform and are proud of it, and one of the favourite
suggestions made by mistresses and maids has been the

formation of a corps of skilled domestic workers with their
own regulation dress. We cannot feel that the cap
represents one of the real hardships of service.

(vi.) PROSPECTS.—The prospects of the domestic servant
are often held out as an inducement to parents and working-
class girls. A capable servant has, at present, practical
certainty of employment for many years of her life, with
prospects of advancement according to her own initiative.
The fourteen-year-old betweenmaid has, metaphorically,
a housekeeper's keys of office in the tin trunk which holds
her first outfit. Domestic service probably offers more
" prizes " than most callings open to the efficient working-
woman, whose parents have not been able to pay for
expensive training in her girlhood, provided she possesses
the rather special temperament to which domestic service
is congenial. But, apart from the prizes, two points must
be noted with regard to the future of the average servant.
First : the demand for responsible elder servants, housekeepers, upper-parlourmaids, upper-housemaids, does not
nearly equal the supply of them. We give in illustration
statistics kindly supplied by one very large and well-
known servants' registry :—

ONE YEAR'S APPLICANTS.

	Percentage of Employees to Employers.	
	Employees.	Employers.
Housekeepers	294	100
Working Housekeepers	228	100
Upper Housemaids	172	100
Useful Maids	172	100
Thorough Maids	166	100
Job Cooks at 15s.	157	100
Children's Maids	158	100
Stillroom Maids	139	100
Nurses at £25 and over	125	100
Upper Parlourmaids	125	100
Job Parlourmaids	114	100
Job Cooks, 14s. a week	113	100
Job Cooks, 16s. and over	117	100

Second : the Census and Board of Trade returns show
a marked diminution of servants after forty years old.
There were in 1911 (in round numbers), 300,000 women

servants aged from twenty-five to thirty-five; 135,000 between thirty-five and forty-five; and 126,000 aged from forty-five to sixty-five (see census returns, quoted in Appendix vi.).

These two sets of figures indicate : (a) that it is hard for the middle-aged servant, even if efficient, to get good fresh employment, in which experience, rather than physical freshness tells ; and (b) that the third or fourth-rate servant tends to get squeezed out of service altogether in middle age. Perhaps, as things are at present, domestic service offers more hope to the inefficient when they are young than do other industrial pursuits. The private employer will put up with mistakes which would be insupportable in the competitive world of business ; and either the mistress or upper servants can, by much labour of superintendence, just keep such workers going. But after years of scoldings and changes of situations, the incompetent servant either dislikes the whole business too much to stick to it, or she finds that she cannot get any situation that is even passably good, and drifts away.

What does the ex-servant do if she leaves the world of domestic service ? In the majority of cases she marries, in which case her home will almost certainly measure the level of domestic service to which she belonged. Though this is not an industrial aspect of service, its advantage or otherwise as a preparation for married life cannot be neglected. It is one of the traditional merits of service. " Think what a help it will be to you to have been in service when you have a home of your own." How many times has this been said to reluctant damsels shrinking from leaving home for their first situation !

The employers consulted by the Women's Industrial Council, many of them well known social workers in town and country, replied that the outstanding advantage of domestic service was its preparation for being head of a household, and that any visitor to the home of a good servant would know what her employment before marriage had been from the appearance of her house and children. From north, south, east and west, town and country correspondents were all unanimous about this. The only exceptions made were in the case of the very inefficient servant, whose inborn inefficiency would not be terminated by marriage, and the ultra-efficient, such as the specialised lady's maid, or the high-class parlourmaid, who would have little experience of spending on the scale of an artisan's wages, and might be ill-fitted for a working-man's home. But, as one Scotch maid observed about this, an intelligent woman could soon adapt her way of living to actual needs.

What possibilities does domestic service afford of earning wages after marriage, either to the widow, or to the wife whose husband cannot work or earn enough for the family ? Correspondents from every part of the country replied with unanimity that the former servant can readily get stop-gap work of some sort—though it was much to be deprecated that she should have to go out to work in her husband's lifetime ; that in most villages occasional help from a labourer's wife who had had good domestic training was welcomed ; that in industrial towns a former servant, especially if she knew how to cook, would be thankfully employed ; but that in residential towns there was generally a great over-supply of charwomen[1] and of unsatisfactory daily servants, though married women who would go out altogether would, if otherwise competent, obtain work just as readily as the unmarried. Such regular work, however, involves, in the case of a widow, breaking up the home. Employers will occasionally allow one child to be brought to a situation by a widowed mother ; but the expense of paying for boarding out children generally far outweighs the superior earnings of domestic service.

Service has this advantage over industrial occupations, to those who return to it late in life, that it is *the* conservative trade. The worker coming back to it will not find herself at loss through a change of process, as may always be the case in factory work. Also domestic service represents a universal want ; the worker, if employed at all, is not tied to a special locality as in some factory work. For the woman who is supplementing husband's or children's

---

[1] The Census statistics of 1911, which gives the total numbers of charwomen as 126,000 (of whom 100,000 in round numbers were married or widowed) obviously cannot account for the armies of women anxious for part-time employment in charing.

earnings, or out-relief, by one or two days' charing per week, training in domestic service is a definite financial asset, though opinions will differ as to the advantages of this supplementary wage-earning from other points of view. But for the woman who has to be mainly dependent for the support of others on her earnings in domestic work it does not compare very favourably with other forms of employment.

The wife who goes out with her husband to one of the "married couple" situations now often available, is apt to have a very hard time. The daily, or supply, servant has generally to start to work early and return late, probably without a half-holiday or a free Sunday, a serious disadvantage to the mother of growing children. This is a great difficulty in the way of organising daily service for reliable married women and widows, for which, otherwise, there would in many towns be definite scope.

It must be remembered that this question of after-employment affects differently the woman who was in upper-class or in lower-class service before marriage. Charing is very hard work for the woman accustomed to "good service," and it is only occasionally that a sufficient regular connection can be got for waiting or for evening cooking.

As a whole, the ex-servant is probably in a better position than the former factory hand, both for supplementing the family earnings in emergency, and for looking after her household ; but, *cæteris paribus*, she is in a decidedly less good position all round if she and her children have to be entirely or mainly dependent on her earnings.

The following are the comments of a Midland factory worker on certain suggested criticisms of servants' prospects :—

"Daily service is too tying after marriage. In the factory the married women are allowed out to look after the meals in most cases. In daily service there is no change whatever in a woman's life ; she does not want all housework, and in these cases it is the woman's home that suffers.

" ' A servant has no trade after marriage.' Up in the North there is a good demand for daily service : there are so many works where girls are employed that even after marriage the servant can easily find work.

" ' A servant has less opportunity for marriage.' Living in a manufacturing town we always think that servants stand a good chance of marriage. We shall have to break down these petty class distinctions, and hope it will help us to realise that all labour is honourable. We are being educated at present by being made to realise that we all depend on each other, and I think we shall soon have learned the lesson.

"'A servant is less well-adapted for a working-class home after marriage.' Am afraid the buying would be on a much larger scale than she would have to practise after marriage."

Below are given three answers to the question, " Would you advise a young friend to go to service ? "

A temporary daily servant, at 10s. a week, aged twenty-five; hours 10–6 :—

" No : because if a girl has a business she has more time to herself where a domestic in most cases is never done. Also should she marry and have reverses she can take up her own business."

A cook-general :—

" No, not if there was any chance of taking up anything else. A trade in the hands is a great help to a woman if she falls into unfortunate circumstances later on in life."

A cook, aged thirty-eight, £20 a year :—

" No, because I think it better to learn a trade if possible : it would be of much more use should they get married and have to work again, as charing and washing are very hard work and not very well paid."

If they do not marry, are elderly servants or ex-servants worse off than other women-workers of the industrial class ? It is worth while to ask this question, because of the very common belief that a larger proportion of servants than of their friends and relatives in other occupations remain unmarried. This is probably true of servants as a whole, though it is not necessarily a case of *post hoc, propter hoc* ; and members of their own class and scores of kindly employers wrote to say how anxious respectable working-men generally seemed to be to secure domestic servants if possible as wives.

The younger " superior " servant now sometimes becomes a sick-nurse, in which case she is at once transported to a different social grade. And she sometimes becomes assistant or working matron at a girls' or children's training home, which, probably, provides her with human interests but a low rate of pay. Most small charitable institutions can at present give only low salaries to their workers. But the difficulty of obtaining suitable under-matrons is so great that it seems clear that institutions will have perforce to offer more often an economic wage, at least to their " working " assistants. If this were done it would be worth while to organise short courses of special training for such workers. Have the possibilities of recruiting for this very valuable but much under-staffed and under-paid form of employment been sufficiently considered ?

There are three main courses open to the elderly unmarried servant :—

(1) She may invest her savings in starting a lodging-house, probably in partnership with a friend. There are, so far as one can guess, too many lodgings to let in the country, and the management of a house is both hard and anxious work. But it may procure a very good livelihood and independence to a capable woman with some initiative. Hundreds of servants do so invest their savings yearly.

(2) She may retire and keep house for a relative, probably in return for her board and lodging. A number of former servants wrote from such peaceful havens.

(3) She may be squeezed out of service, probably when between fifty and sixty years of age. If—and this often happens—she has no relations or friends' homes near to her, her prospects are very dismal. For a time she can live on her savings ; several mistresses produced instances of servants who, by early middle age, had saved £100 in well-to-do, not rich, families ; a few who have been in good service will have liberal pensions from employers ; but most —and especially those rolling stones who have been in poor service, and have frequently changed their places— have little to hope from this, and it is very difficult for them to get along between the age at which they lose their work and that at which the State Pension begins. Some may get charing work ; probably there were many ex-servants among the 10,500 unmarried women who were included in the 72,500 charwomen whom the census returns of 1911 scheduled as between forty-five years old and " seventy-five and upwards." But their lot is hardly enviable. Workhouse statistics could give much information as to the fate of these elderly women, for whom, even

if part of their suffering is due to their own fault or folly, one cannot but be truly sorry.

An upper-housemaid aged forty-one, in service since ten years old, wages £30, writes :—

" Service is all right when one is young ; in fact, I think a girl would be better off in service, especially if she has not got a home, rather than in business. It's when you get older things get irksome."

A cook-general ; in service since sixteen :—

" I went to service because I have never had a home ; no parents to look after me ; never seen them ; I am nobody's child and never have been. I am old enough to look after myself now. . . .

" If we had kinder mistresses we should love service.

" I shall be so pleased if you could help us who are getting old, too old for service. Mistresses are wanting young girls now. There are many living on dry bread at the Servants' Homes, can't get work —too old for the mistresses.

" I think if the servants had better food and better money we should be much happier. Some poor girls have to work very hard and have very little food. We shall be so pleased if you could help us middle-aged (ones) : the mistresses are wanting young girls now. Could you help us instead of going to the workhouse ? I shall be so pleased if you will."

Perhaps it may be more possible in the future than in the past for the average servant to make provision for the time when she begins to get past work. Compulsory Health Insurance will safeguard her at least against some of the expense of illness. About one per cent. of all who replied to the Council's enquiry appeared to have made such provision by voluntarily joining a Friendly or Collecting Society before the National Insurance Act was passed. It is to be hoped that a superannuation allowance scheme, such as has been already suggested by the Domestic Servants' Insurance Society, may before long become feasible.[1]

[1] This society has drawn up a scheme of provision for old age, as one of the additional benefits for which its members may subscribe, after paying the State contribution for provision against sickness, etc., under Part I. of the Insurance Act. Thus a member can get a pension commencing at the age of 60, going on until the age of 70 and then continuing at a half rate, when it can be supplemented by the State Pension. The amount of the Pension can be anything from 2/6 to £1 per week, and will be paid weekly when the member reaches the age of 60.

Some examples are as follows :—

A member joining at the age of 20 can get a pension of 5/- a week by paying 6/5½ a quarter.

A member joining at the age of 25 can get a pension of 7/6 a week by paying 12/4½ a quarter.

A member joining at the age of 30 can get a pension of 10/- a week by paying £1 1s. a quarter.

Earnings of servants might be made to go further by more training in thrift. Servants quite naturally often tend to be extravagant in expenditure and many employers of young servants do not realize their responsibility for inculcating the dismal virtue. A bonus on savings is a laudable way of sugaring the pill for the quite young maid. Also, servants could put by more if their relatives made fewer claims on them. " Almost every servant that I ever knew has had some one dependent on her," wrote many mistresses and maids. The generosity to her family of the good daughter in service is one of her very best points, and the prospects of such future help are sometimes an inducement to parents to let their children enter service. While no one wishes to cut the servant off from this connection with her family, yet, as a matter of fact, existing legislation is tending that way. The evils of sickness, accident and unemployment in certain trades are now greatly diminished, while the poor-law provides for the necessities of the very poor, and multitudes of sources of voluntary aid offer their help. This may be good or bad for the social and family life of the community as a whole ; but it means, quite definitely, that servants will in the future be less responsible than in the past for acting as buffers to their families in financial distress. Also wages are being raised by law and by combination, and there will be progressively less need for low family wages to be supplemented by the daughter away from home, though the necessity is far from being at an end yet.

Industrial prospects are, on the average, probably rather better in domestic service than in most of even the better trades. But the average prospects in domestic service are struck between widely different extremes, varying from the old servant trying to rejoice over Brabazon work in the workhouse to the respected " family treasure " pensioned, with her own rooms in her employer's home, or the capable head of comfortable lodgings. There is no reason why these prospects in later life should not be raised as a whole : (a) by organisation of (part time) employment for the middle-aged widowed servant or the wife with others dependent on her; (*b*) by a well-planned scheme of superannuation provision for the old servant.

II—ORGANISATION

(i.) ENTRY. THE PROBLEM OF THE BEGINNER.—As a rule, the industrial position of a trade is measured by the ease or difficulty with which it is entered. Competition and artificial regulation tend in practice to make the process of entering and learning a good trade hard, although it is now beginning to be admitted that such exclusiveness is unwholesome, and that the more free the entry the better will the worker and his trade flourish.

Domestic service suffers both from the ease and the difficulty with which it is entered. On the one hand there is the well-worn reproach that " anyone can be a servant." This is nearly true in the present state of supply and demand, and the knowledge that almost any young woman with even a moderate amount of health and honesty (and cleanliness) can get some kind of " place," more than any other factor lowers the industrial status of servants. Unfortunately it is the lower type of servant, the ill-trained or defective girl, pictured as perpetually cleaning doorsteps, with smuts on her face, that in industrial towns comes chiefly before the eyes of most artisan fathers and their Standard VII. daughters. These are apt to turn aside with contempt from such an occupation, and seek employers with a higher standard of efficiency than this and less demand for " menial work." At the same time there is often real difficulty in entering " good " service, in which the financial prospects and demand for trained intelligence are higher than those in most women's trades. The fluctuating well-to-do household gives less opportunity for good training now than in more stay-at-home days, and when practical teaching is to be had the process is apt to involve a good deal more sacrifice of the things for which the normal girl cares than do most forms of industrial training. To some extent this is inevitable if quite young girls are to go to service ; but the difficulty of the first start arises largely because service is *the* unorganised industry, or group of industries, and this could be greatly lessened by reasonable care.

What is the present process of entering service ? The future domestic servants, like their contemporaries destined to shop or factory, leave school at fourteen, sometimes, unfortunately, at thirteen ; in a small proportion of cases at fifteen. Most girls before leaving school have now had some " domestic " training, varying from the sewing which is part of the universal elementary school curriculum, and probably a weekly cooking class in their last school year, to the ingenious schemes described in Appendix i.

The next step depends on the neighbourhood in which they live and on the social position of their parents. The country girl still often goes out straight from school to a " living-in " place, sometimes to a very rough and hard place, as general in some struggling shopkeeper's or clerk's household in the nearest town ; sometimes to be treated as one of the family under a working mistress ; sometimes, but less often, as between-maid under other servants. Such places are heard of through the smaller registries, through recommendation and private enquiry, and still more by advertisement in the local papers. The industrial success of village girls depends almost entirely on their home training and on their first start out from home. Some villages are fortunate enough to possess a kindly resident who is ready to give a few months' preliminary training on the spot to successive fourteen-year-olds, or to make the enquiries that end in a girl being well started elsewhere. Working-class parents, especially when struggling to make both ends meet, are apt to ask surprisingly inadequate questions as to their daughters' places in service. It has been for generations the traditional task of the squire's or clergyman's wife to supply such information, while the Girls' Friendly Society has, for nearly forty years, volunteered to find " safe " first places whenever possible, and to keep in touch with country girls after they are placed.

It is said that there is a growing tendency among village girls to stay at home and not " go out to work." While it may be desirable for them if they have good homes to defer their start as wage-earners until they are fifteen or sixteen, yet with the majority of agricultural labourers' daughters the existing level of their parents' wages and

housing accommodation makes it better for them to leave
home quite early.

Two points stand out in considering the entry of the
village girl to service.

(1) Rural depopulation has tapped the source from which
the great majority of servants came, but the demand for
them has risen. Hence come the circulars sent round to
some villages by London registry offices, and the facilities
offered by the " domestic " advertisements of many newspapers. Hence, too, the need for help by public authorities,
by voluntary societies (and thousands of young country
servants have reason to be grateful to the Girls' Friendly
Society), and by individuals in bringing together good
employers and good girls. Although in many villages girls
are successfully started out by their parents with,
perhaps, occasional help from a neighbour, yet there
is clearly room, even in the country, for some rather
more definite organisation for placing girls under seventeen
in service.

(2) Country girls, like town girls, are now less ready than
in the past to go to service. But, unlike town girls, they
have seldom any industrial alternative.[1] It seems clear
that better domestic training should be given to them, as
to their town cousins, just before or after leaving school,
so that the first stages of wage-earning should be less un-
pleasant than they often are at present. In some cases,
but not very many, help has to be arranged for the provision
of the outfit. Most little village girls would probably be

[1] Replies to the question, " Why did you go to service ? "
" My father was a shepherd at 13/- a week."
" My father was a farm-labourer with a large family and there was
nothing else to do."
" We live in the country ; my father died, and I had no choice."
" I lived in the country : my father had to keep nine of us on 13/-
a week."
" My father was a shepherd. I was the fifth of twelve and had to go
out at fifteen (now at thirty-one a cook at £25) ; no choice . . . we
lived in the country."
" There were ten in the family—we lived in a village, so I had
to go."
" We lived in a village. I always wanted to go to service, and, I am
afraid, I admired the servants' clothes when they came home for their
holiday."
" There is nothing else for one to do in the country except go to
service."

quite willing to go to service and to settle down there if a guiding hand were ready to help them.

The town girl who goes into service generally comes from the residential towns, or from the suburbs of manufacturing towns where conditions are fairly similar. She has been brought up in one of two very clearly marked social classes ; (1) the labouring class, for whom the alternative to service is rough factory work, beginning at a weekly wage of from three to six shillings, normally five shillings, as compared with two to three shillings and keep in a first place ; and (2) the artisan class, which sends girls to shops and offices, to workrooms, and the best sort of factory work, where the initial earnings are generally lower than in service. A certain proportion of these town girls go out to service at once ; there were 39,000 thirteen- and fourteen-year-olds returned as domestic servants in the census of 1911. But there is a clearly marked tendency on the part of parents to put off their daughters' start-out in life till they are fifteen at least, though the influence of the National Insurance Act has been pulling against this among small employers. It will be interesting to see which force predominates. A girl who does not go out straight as a little general either stays at home for a year and "helps mother" —and in the case of an eldest daughter leaving school, such help may mean the only remission of toil which the mother has had for fourteen years—or she may take out a baby, or get a place as morning girl in a three- or four-servant household, where the shortage of servants has made it possible for the cook and housemaid to insist on half-day help in their work. Girls from very poor homes often go out as servants by the day, working in a small house from seven a.m. to eight or nine p.m. at 1/6 to 3/- and meals. At fifteen or sixteen these day-girls start out, either as generals or as between-girls or under-housemaids, having got their clothes together and learnt some rudiments of household work. Some defer the start to seventeen or eighteen, or even older ; either because their parents like them to learn dressmaking as a preparation for the greatly overstocked calling of ladies' maids and sewing-maids, or because they started at factory work and only entered service as "generals" when disillusioned. One well-

known factory in an industrial part of London was described to us as run thus by the labour of young girls who,
at seventeen or eighteen, were turned off and perforce
entered service of some sort.[1]

Is the entry satisfactory from the point of view of the
girl or her possible employer ? Not on the whole. On
the one hand, the young beginner in service often has an
unnecessarily hard time, though the well-brought-up girl
in a good first place may sail in smooth waters. It is true
that some hardships are often good for the self-satisfied
young person, fresh from school successes and from the
normal indulgence of home. But she is apt to have an
excessive number of difficulties—much more than meet her
brother at the same age, whether he is learning a trade or
running errands. This is due partly to lack of consideration on the part of the mistress and still more of the other
servants ; partly to want of organisation in the household,
so that the youngest servant may degenerate into a child
charwoman or a perpetual dish-washer. On the other
hand the beginner is often both inefficient and unwilling
to be taught, and many of her trials are due to her own
incompetence. Methods of education have made a great
gap between the old-fashioned servant and the young girl,
and mistresses often find their elder maids unwilling to give
training ; while if, as too often happens now, the upper
servants themselves change their places yearly, they
obviously cannot be expected to take much trouble over
the under girls.

Many remedies have been suggested, both in the direction
of improved efficiency and better conditions.

With regard to efficiency the following suggestions have
been made :—

(1) The revival or development of a system of domestic

[1] Of the servants who replied to the Women's Industrial Council's
circular,

6 per cent. started service at twelve.			
11	,,	,,	,,	thirteen.
23	,,	,,	,,	fourteen.
17	,,	,,	,,	fifteen.
12	,,	,,	,,	sixteen.
10	,,	,,	,,	seventeen.
7	,,	,,	,,	eighteen.
6	,,	,,	,,	twenty-five and over.

apprenticeship, by which girls should be bound to selected mistresses for two or three years, and should be well taught in every way. This is very good in theory ; but it is entirely against the spirit of the age. Formal apprenticeship for boys does not survive in those trades in which they can learn as much without. Still less would it be likely to flourish in the case of girls, whose industrial career will probably be cut short by marriage. The suggestion re-appears in a changed form in this proposal :—

(2) The establishment by the County Council or Munici-pality of lists of mistresses who are ready to train girls under reasonable conditions.

This is being done already on a small scale. The officials of every agency for befriending girls have, at least, a mental list of ladies to whom it is always safe to send girls for first places. The registries of the Girls' Friendly Society specialise in this, which might well be developed and centralised by the new Juvenile Advisory and Juvenile Employment Committees.

Having established such a schedule, the corollary often suggested is : " Send girls straight into service at fourteen, before they have begun to want their evenings out." This is the old-fashioned remedy for the dearth of servants. It is quite true that the year (or two years) after leaving school is often at present nearly wasted ; but the remedy suggested will not suit all cases, however careful mistresses may be. The stunted child of four feet ten inches and under, whom not all the efforts of parents and medical inspectors and care committees have developed ; the deli-cate girl from the comfortable artisan home—these are not in the least fitted for domestic service at fourteen. If they do find situations they are apt to become hopeless little drudges, in constant hot water with either the mistress or the older servants. Service at fourteen may be very satisfactory for some strong girls, and even, sometimes, for undersized and incompetent children if they are under kind mistresses or upper maids. All honour should be given to such trainers, who are by no means universal. But in any case, girls who go straight into service at fourteen are apt to lose all their former outside attachments— friends, Sunday school or Bible class, etc. In some cases, but of course not all, this change of surroundings is most valuable for a child brought up in a bad or doubtful home.

(3) A third very favourite panacea is "More domestic training at school." On the one side, employers may say cheerily that half or the whole of the school time of all " working-class " girls over ten should be spent in domestic work, and some practical-minded parents would welcome this ; on the other, enthusiasts for literary education cry out against calling down too soon the " shades of the prison house," and entreat that the curriculum should not be made too utilitarian. A compromise seems quite possible. All normal girls who leave school at thirteen or fourteen should have some definite domestic training, just as secondary school girls should be so trained, preferably with a view to making them able to look after their own homes, since the fundamentals of household work are the same. Older girls, now often bored by school after thirteen, would gain greatly in most cases by much more practical work than is supplied by a weekly cooking lesson, especially if such work were correlated with their other lessons. They should benefit both from the educational and the utilitarian point of view. The Board of Education is taking steps in this direction, but effective training involves expense in the provision of apparatus and of teachers, and from this local authorities shrink. Various education committees are, however, making experiments in domestic, as in other forms of manual teaching, and much is to be hoped from their development. One of the best schemes so far is that which turns selected elementary school girls from poor districts for, perhaps, three days a week, into a furnished cottage or " domestic centre " equipped in the same way, for practical training in " housewifery." No one would say that thirteen is the ideal age for such training, but there seems little alternative at present. The problem of domestic service would, or might, be greatly simplified if the school leaving age were raised to fifteen. There are many valid objections to this under present educational conditions, but it would remove the existing difficulty that the possible servants of the future generally leave school before they are old enough for service, while nearly a year may elapse before they can

make effective use of any " domestic " teaching that they have received.

(4) After-school Education. Allowing that most girls only take preliminary places at fourteen, and that many lose ambition ever to rise above these, what can be done to stop the present wastage of good material ? It is at this period that technical training for domestic service, as such, is greatly wanted if it is to be raised, as it should be, to the level of a skilled trade.

Such technical training could be given in three ways :— (a) by Continuation Classes for girls between fourteen and sixteen, who are in day places or are marking time at home—classes definitely for young servants, held with the co-operation of employers two or three times a week in the afternoon or early evening. Such classes have been held with success in Switzerland and Germany. They may not accomplish very much in actual instruction, but they would raise the status of the young domestic worker, just as that of the telegraph boys has been raised by similar classes, and they would give incentive to improvement to the girls in rough, small places and to those with the not very engrossing occupation of wheeling out a baby's perambulator. Such classes should be quite easily started in towns, though their organisation would involve a good deal of hard work in securing the sympathy of employers and parents and the interest of the girls.

(b) By Day Training, on the principle of the London County Council Trade Schools. At present these have not done very much for service, though they are being developed in this direction.[1] They should appeal to girls from the well-to-do artisan class, but they are, of course, very costly, though old endowments in some cases could lessen the burden on the rates and taxes.

(c) By Residential Training for periods of three to six months or one year or, perhaps, two or more years.

Appendix i. summarises the different ways in which residential training is being given (i.) by training homes of every type and by poor law and industrial schools ; (ii.) by County Council and Municipal training schemes ;

[1] See Appendix i. for such work in different centres.

(iii.) by the Women's Industrial Council in the Nursery Training School.

Really well-trained girls, taught under either of the two latter systems, should do much to raise the status of servants in the future if their training were free from the reproach, now sometimes levied against it, that its products are given over to theories, and are too " efficient " to condescend to the mere potato-peeling and dish-washing which form so large a part of all domestic work. This is clearly a possible danger, but one that ought to be readily avoidable.

We return to our first two points, or platitudes : that if the entry to the trade is to be satisfactory, both its conditions must be improved for the sake of the beginner, and the beginner's efficiency must be improved for the sake of the employer. Perhaps we should add that the conditions and prospects of service as a whole should be improved, if good beginners are to enter and remain in service.

The first can be, to a great extent, achieved by propaganda work among employers. Nothing better could be done for service as a calling than the raising of the normal conditions of entry even approximately to those already provided by the really good employer or good servant. In no denunciation of service should the long-sufferance shown by uncounted motherly mistresses of silly little maids be neglected. Here is the opportunity for the different societies connected with girls—the Girls' Friendly Society, Metropolitan Association for Befriending Young Servants, the Working Women's Guilds and all the scattered training homes—to coalesce and recommend some common standard of treatment, training and efficiency. The main justification of the attempt to sweep domestic service into the Labour Exchange system, under the ægis of Juvenile Advisory or Juvenile Employment Committees, is surely this, that it gives for the first time an opportunity for an impartial authority to insist on some serious attention to the needs both of the young maid and of her employer.

The second can be brought about largely by improved education, in the widest sense, and not by technical training only. In few forms of work does character tell as it does in service. More than one experienced mistress and head of a training home wrote to the effect that it was much better from the point of view of both employer and employed that a maid should be willing and teachable rather than well-trained and opinionative. Employers who care about their workpeople often speak in the same way about their boy-workers—saying that while technical teaching is, on the whole, most desirable, yet the learned paragon from such a school may be not nearly so likely to succeed in the workshop as the more commonplace boy who is adaptable and will use common-sense. Obviously this is still more necessary in the close contact brought about by domestic service. The reformers of domestic service cannot therefore exalt efficiency at the expense of character. But there is no reason against cultivating both.

A detailed summary of what is being done towards preparation for service is given at page 109 of this book. What we want to urge is that such preparation should be considered seriously, from the national point of view ; and also that it is not of much use to improve the beginnings of domestic service, and to spend much time and trouble in training girls for it unless at the same time its later stages are correspondingly improved on the part of employers.

The following are extracts from servants' replies giving their early experiences in service.

A housekeeper-general, with twenty-four years' experience, entered service at fifteen years old :—

"I look back with many regrets to my first place on account of poor and insufficient food. I was a strong, robust girl, but my health got completely ruined and have never been as strong since."

A very misanthropic house-parlourmaid in a fashionable part of London : placed out in service at fifteen and a half by an association after one month's training in a Home on her father's death :—

"Take the young girl who comes out from some orphanage or industrial school, what does she know of service in a general way ? . . . it is usually the retired tradesman and his wife and far v . . . a house in some London suburb, who engages these innocent girls and makes them work from morn till night without a break often. In many cases these ladies (so-called) are not educated themselves, and do not know what household management is. Then how can they train those girls ? When anything goes wrong the

blame is put on the maid. They slave—for what ? They are
expected to cook, wash, do housework, for the magnificent sum of
£8 a year, perhaps."

A Scotch lady's maid :—

" Much ought to be done to encourage young girls and boys, who
enter service when they leave school or soon after : many of them
come from happy homes (even if they be poor homes) and in service
they find things totally different and receive many a shock in the
bullying, unkind and often sulky manner in which they are treated
by their ' superiors,' who oftentimes forget the hard times they had
to experience themselves.   In many cases one sees the character
and disposition of young girls and boys entirely ruined by the intem-
perate habits, filthy and immoral conversation of those over them.
If they are not bullied into doing their work and ' staying on,' they
get discouraged and leave their situation, take another, find that
a failure, then in sheer desperation degenerate into a ' little
general,' etc."

A cook, now earning £28 as a general ; began when fifteen
years old :—

" I started domestic service in a very large house with a great
many servants, including men.   In my own case I was overworked,
not through the wish of the mistress, who was an excellent mistress,
but through being put upon by other servants.   I have suffered
through that ever since.   I believe that is a very common evil in
large houses."

A general servant, £15 a year, after twenty years in
service :—

" I had no training whatever : lost my mother at the age of ten
years ; had to be at work at thirteen years of age ; my first place
was a very hard one.   There were eight in family, and a four-
storied house to keep clean, which was the first starting of ruin of
my health.   I had no outfit ; had to do the best with what I had,
because I had no home."

An under-kitchenmaid in a castle, aged twenty-one ;
wages, £18 :—

" I would not advise any young friend to go into service, especially
not in the kitchen, because while girls are under, it is nothing short
of slavery. . . . I think girls in service ought to have just certain
hours' work, the same as shop girls, although the head servants
make places what they are for under ones, in most cases."

An ex-factory hand, now acting as companion help.
Nine years in service :—

" From my own experience of domestic service I can't see why
more girls don't go.   I think it helps to fetch out of most girls what

F

is best in them, as they see things differently and it makes them more broad-minded, and yet I don't think they have the love for home when they go to service so young. I am sure if I was a mother I would not think of sending a child of mine until she was about nineteen or twenty."

" Of course it is much better for girls without a good home, but I think I should prefer to see them learn a good trade, or if possible stay at school a year or two longer, and then go into an office."

A cook, with twenty-three years' experience :—

" Make service less like a prison, especially to the young beginners, for they are generally home-sick, and staying in for a whole week frightens them, and they seek the factory or any work where they can return to their homes of an evening. Service is much the best to the girl who has no home, or a bad one, and if she gets with a good mistress is much better off than in a factory. I think whatever branch of service a girl ought to be trained for it : she can command better money, and is much more independent and can pick and choose her situation."

(ii.) A STANDARD OF EFFICIENCY.—Is there a standard of efficiency in domestic service comparable to the standard stereotyped for most trades by custom and combination ? There are very definite standards in the minds of most mistresses and maids, and these to a limited extent become common property. The thoroughly competent maid and mistress are admirable and most versatile workers, whose efficiency is only less easy to measure than is that of the industrial worker or manager because, in economic phrase, it produces utilities not commodities. But the really capable and well-equipped head of a household is by no means universal, while the perfectly efficient maid is rare enough to be expensive. Below these there is no general standard, and efficiency is measured only by isolated opinions.

All the mistresses circularised by the Women's Industrial Council were consulted about means of raising the alleged low industrial status of domestic service. Almost all gave inefficiency as one of the root causes of this ; and readily admitted that mistress and maid were often equally incompetent.

A whole series of remedies and suggestions was offered on this point, and as these appear constantly in conversation and in newspapers they may be summarised as follows :—

(a) There is great need of more interest than at present in domestic subjects, and of more facilities for training the employing classes in them. " Let woman return to her proper sphere." There has undoubtedly been a decided recrudescence of interest during the last decade in household management reflected in varying degrees from the courses lately inaugurated at King's College to " Our Housewife's Corner " in the women's weeklies and the parish magazines. But it seems to be felt that more chances of training are wanted, especially for those who cannot spare time for courses in the residential training colleges. Not nearly enough secondary schools contrive to include " domestic subjects " in their crowded curricula, whereas this should be universal, if possible. (b) A few correspondents indeed pointed out with much truth that the good management of a household was quite as much a result of general intelligence as of specialised education ; and that the university woman or the artist or musician could become a particularly good housekeeper if she chose. (c) Others said that practice at home was more important than anything else ; that a well-to-do mother should make all her children, boys and girls equally, take some share in household work—including, according to one lady, at least a week's unaided work in the scullery ; and that mistresses or their daughters should have moral courage enough at least occasionally to face the servants and cook in their own kitchens.

It is true that neither the possession of special training nor general intelligence will make every possible head of a household successful. The home, or at least its practical management, is *not* the sphere of all women. Many people in all classes do not want to be domestic. If they are rich they can escape to hotels. If they are poor or have children who cannot be fitted into hotel life, it ought to be possible for such women to combine, as is being now done in America, for co-operative housekeeping ; a system by which separate homes and family life can be maintained, but the worry of providing food and looking after the needs of a household can be centralised. This is not at all a universal remedy ; many people would greatly dislike it ; but it would clearly save the community much time and temper and trouble that are at present wasted, both on the part of the woman who is normally held responsible, and of her family on whom her failures react. Meanwhile the desirability of further training for most well-to-do girls remains. Some servants who were consulted in the matter agreed that it would be excellent if mistresses could be trained in household work, so that they might know how much it was fair to expect the maids to do. Some on the other hand, said that it was much better for mistresses to get competent servants and leave all to them. Obviously, the need for detailed knowledge of household work varies in different types and sizes of household; but equally obviously, some knowledge is most desirable, even if you can afford the most competent of housekeepers.

Servants' inefficiency, on the other hand is, of course, a constant cause of complaint, not so much in the rich family which can afford to pay high wages and insist on good service in return, as in the three, two and one-servant households. These have continually to put up with incompetent servants; incompetent partly because they know that the prizes of the profession are not for them and there is no industrial incentive to improvement; partly because, like other woman workers, they are apt to be unambitious, and are sure that they will marry. Probably better household equipment, with the use of labour-saving devices and part time daily service, will progressively reduce the very real troubles of these households.

Meanwhile there is immense room for improvement in the quality of the middle and lower ranks of domestic service, such as the different forms of training summarised in the previous section should secure or advance. The steady influx of even a moderate number of well-trained and intelligent recruits to the ranks of domestic service should do much to raise its industrial standard as a whole. But valuable though good training must be, there is a good deal of truth in two comments made equally by experienced mistresses and servants; (a) that efficiency in service depends much more on method that comes from practice and common-sense than on actual technique such as can be taught in formal classes; (b) that character and good sense are more important than actual skill in the

great majority of situations. " Efficiency " in domestic
service has a more comprehensive meaning than in the
trades, and must be sought by a much greater variety of
means.

(iii.) FINDING PLACES AND SERVANTS.—Both mistresses
and maids were asked by the Women's Industrial Council
for their views about servants' registries. Almost all with
any knowledge of the subject agreed that registries, if they
are to continue, need licensing (and supervising) as has been
done by the London County Council, and by various local
authorities. It was urged that licensing should be made
compulsory and not, as at present, permissive, as a condition of existence. Further, as several correspondents
pointed out, such licensing may be useless and even dangerous unless at the same time the local authority frames
rules, and passes by-laws for their regulation.[1] Recent
correspondence has drawn much attention to the possible
evils of the unlicensed registry ; but while a good deal has
been done, some local authorities are unaccountably slack
in taking any steps in the matter. Even by-laws cannot
make any registry system, private or national, perfect.
A number of those who wrote of the question asked per-
tinently—How supervise ? With regard to existing methods
of making engagements there were very different opinions,
equally among servants and mistresses. The majority
denounced registries, but often gave no reason at all for
doing so. Their replies often seemed only to represent the
normal attitude of criticism towards all established institutions which demand money for possible services.

Some correspondents said without hesitation that
registries are very good. This was said especially with
regard to three or four large and well-known offices, and to
little country registries with local interest and knowledge.
It is clear that there are far too many medium-sized registries
in the country, both for the work that they can do and for
their own financial success ; it is these—which offer neither
the large choice of the first-class registries nor the minute
knowledge of the small, old-fashioned offices—that lead to
the unpopularity of the present registry system. It is with

[1] See Appendix iii. for specimen by-laws.

regard to these that servants sometimes complain bitterly that the managers do not know or explain about situations ; they send them without warning to a lady who has had five cooks in six weeks, while equally they supply a careful mistress with a maid who (with or without their knowledge) has never been known to stay more than a month with any recent employer. These stories get exaggerated ; but such discontent is at least in part the product of the present system. Unless you can get full references on both sides (which the commercial registry can hardly ever do) even good registries may bring together quite incompatible mistresses and maids, while unprincipled registrars have many temptations for doing so ; and because of our " character " system such misfits tend on the whole to bear more hardly on the maid than on the mistress. A few instances were given of registry offices encouraging servants to change places. But obviously nothing of this sort is to their interest, even if frequent changes are temporarily profitable. A number complain of young girl clerks who do most of the interviewing at many large registries. This is not very serious, but there is some ground for sympathy for the middle-aged servant and employer, cross-questioned by them.

If mistresses and maids are discontented with registries there are at present three main alternatives :—

1. To use advertisements. These are becoming more and more widespread, and the use of them is being scientifically organised in many daily and weekly papers.

A very large number of " good " mistresses and maids say they always have advertised and will continue to do so, as it is so much more satisfactory. The method succeeds with grown-up workers, but is not so satisfactory for young maids or boy servants, for whom it is almost essential to have an intermediary unless an interview and personal information about a new situation can be secured.

2. The second alternative is to nationalise the registries— that is, to supersede them by Labour Exchanges or to subordinate them to the latter.

About fifteen per cent. of the mistresses who replied were anxious for this. Others who agreed in the abstract said that times—and the Exchanges—were not nearly ripe for this yet ; if such a step were ever taken, it must be either as a special branch of Exchange work with separate offices for domestics (to avoid the prejudices of some employers and of upper class servants equally), and with specially trained officials ; or else by some system, not yet thought out, of federating the registries under the local Exchange.[1]

3. To start municipal registries, or registries under the joint control of organisations of mistresses or maids or both jointly, and perhaps financed co-operatively. These schemes sound attractive, but neither mistresses nor maids are easy to organise in the mass.

Most, however, were clearly against these last two proposals on many grounds. Some said there was no reason for saddling the taxpayers with such expense, and that the Exchanges would suffer from the same lack of personal interest which even the best registries presented. It was also pointed out that good servants, like good artisans, would not apply readily to the Exchanges, and that altogether these proposals would not work well for either the registries or the Exchanges.

A number of these criticisms seem valid, not permanently but for the present, specially those dealing with the inexperience of the Labour Exchanges and the legitimate claims of the registries. The Exchanges accordingly chose as their first field of effort the supply of the hotel and business class of servants alone.[2]

The finding of places in private service for boys and girls of fourteen, fifteen, or sixteen is a different and very difficult work. Some philanthropic registries and a few private proprietors of registries have done it very well, and taken an almost maternal interest in those whom they have placed. But it is not a profitable business, for low fees are paid on such engagements and are sometimes not exacted at all, and the vagaries of the young worker and his or her employer are peculiarly trying to the mind of any orderly

[1] Since August, 1914, the Labour Exchanges have been empowered to receive applications for and from domestic servants in all branches of service.

[2] For statistics as to " placings " in domestic service by Labour Exchanges, see Appendix v.

registrar.   Yet it is most important for the welfare of these
young people that adequate enquiry should be made into
the places offered to them when " living in " is involved.
Equally it is desirable that their employers should have
suitable young servants selected, if they really mean to do
their duty in training them. All these considerations
justify the State in beginning to take over from the private
registry, and from the advertisement columns of the papers,
the placing of these young workers. This is being done in
those towns where Juvenile Advisory Committees and
Juvenile Employment Committees have appointed domestic
service sub-committees under the dual system which now
deals with juvenile employment in connection with the
Labour Exchanges.

(iv.) REFERENCES.—The matter of a servant's references
proved to be a very vexed question, on which maids (un-
asked) wrote with more apparent interest than mistresses,
who were specially questioned as to their views. It seems
clear that our present reference system bears hardly on
servants in some cases, and at best leaves them with a
sense of insecurity which is never wholesome. Two
propositions were made in the Council's enquiry form in
order to draw comments from mistresses. (1) That a
servant has no legal claim to a character. (2) That a
mistress often finds it difficult to get a true reference to a
servant. To this the majority of mistresses replied that
they never heard of any difficulty in getting references as
to a servant if she was at all good, though they greatly
preferred to rely on a personal interview and verbal
enquiries ; that a refusal to give a character came from a
charitable desire to avoid incriminating a girl who had been
dishonest, or to escape the law of libel, and that in case of
grave difficulty or injustice to a maid, " someone else,"
perhaps the parish clergyman, would always speak for a
girl. They added tnat, for the sake of other mistresses and
servants, no mistress ought to take a servant without a
reference, and that employers are much to blame for giving
untrue characters which are far more often over-favour-
able than over-critical ; that the supply of servants'
characters should be compulsory and privileged. A certain

number suggested the adoption of character-books on the German system, which insures a brief written record of the maid's work and conduct in each successive situation. As a whole, the mistresses consulted did not think the character difficulty very serious except, perhaps, as regards the employers, partly because those who took the trouble to fill up the Council's prolonged enquiry form were probably " good " employers. Servants wrote with much more feeling on the subject. They complained of three things : (a) the loss of a long good " character " by going for a short time, through a registry or an advertisement, to an impossible situation. They either had to stay, with much discomfort, in such a place, or leave and lose a good reference, since many mistresses will only give a " character " once. This was repeated many times in sensible replies from apparently good servants. (b) Loss of a reference through the death of an employer or through his or her absence abroad. There are thoughtless people who leave home without making provision for their servants' future employment. To remedy this, several employers and experienced servants suggested a system of monthly references, while others drew lurid pictures of the friction that would occur in the household if a bad entry were made against the name of a servant who had been unsuccessful in her dinners, or unfortunate in breakages, for a month. (c) Deliberate falsification of character, or withholding it, from " spite." Various bitter complaints were received about this from rather unattractive maids working for the " self-made " type of employer. We may hope that this does not often occur, but obviously it is a possible danger and one for which the servant has at present no remedy. It may, in extreme circumstances, mean complete ruin for her.

A very illiterate cook, with over twenty years' service, wrote from Preston (spelling altered) :—

" I have had no trouble in having a reference from good families. The class of ladies which I find will give no references is the middle class, who had no servants in her younger days—barmaids or school teachers (!) who was raised in the ranks by marriage. These are the class that scout after our references, and will keep us out of work. It will be a boon to do something. In this part of England servants are treated very bad. They think because we are in service, we spent our early days in prison."

There is much to be said for the Irish system, by which the servant has a traditional claim on her mistress for a written statement giving the period during which she was in her service. A series of such statements give, at least, an indication of the type of service in which she has been. It ought to be possible to enforce this, either by custom or by compulsion, and the minimum statement could be supplemented by favourable comments if desired. There is no reason why the servant should not be possessed of a series of written references to past service, such as those which the errand-boy and the migratory agricultural labourer carry in their pockets.

Akin to the question of servants' characters is that of reference as to the mistress. This seems to be becoming a common desire and it is, in many ways, quite reasonable, though few of those who repeat it take the trouble to think out methods by which it could be realised. Servants repeatedly say " so many questions are asked about them, why should not the characters of their employers be investigated also ? " It may mean so very much to a girl, morally as well as industrially, if she goes to the wrong place.

To this democratic suggestion employers replied with an open mind. A certain number said, " No. A servant can always leave in a month if she does not like a place." (This neglects the question of the next reference, and the possibility that a good maid may fall into a wholly undesirable place.) A larger number said, " Such a reference system is quite unnecessary. The young servant should not go far from home ; in which case personal inquiries can be made about a prospective situation, or if she must go to a distance, the long-suffering parish clergyman can always be consulted. Older servants always can and do find out about a place from the tradesmen and other servants." (For this purpose, it was added, the good employer should take pains to ensure that a possible maid has a chance of talking to her present servants.)

This, however, is often impossible now that servants come from long distances and employers move about so much. A servant's decision to take a place often means a leap completely in the dark.

A large proportion of mistresses were quite ready to give references—such as those asked for by the registries of the Girls' Friendly Society—or to let the Labour Exchange or police or some impartial authority hold them, if they held the servants' references too. On principle many made little objection to this ; but they asked, " Who is going to give the reference ? The outgoing between-maid ? "

It ought to be possible, in spite of the obvious difficulties, to think out some system of getting without offence a reference to an unknown employer—a minimum reference as to the " respectability " of the household and wholesome conditions, just as a minimum reference to the servants' past record should always be accessible. In practice, registries often give these verbally ; but there is no means by which the commercial registry can enforce this, and there would be obvious temptations for the unprincipled registry office. All the sensible employers were unanimous on the inadequacy of compulsory, unprivileged characters and, indeed, of any written reference, on either side. People experienced in dealing with testimonials of any kind would probably confirm this. But they give, at least, a basis on which to make further enquiries when these seem desirable ; and the common right to such written reports would remove some of the inequality which does exist in the relationship of employer and employed. The system in practice is often perfectly satisfactory, but its modification would remove the complete dependency on the justice of the individual employer which is irksome to the modern worker.

(v.) DEFINITE TERMS.—" The terms in service should be made definite." This is a frequent suggestion which was offered for the consideration of the mistresses circularised. Most of these replied to the effect that they knew of no indefiniteness, except in minor details ; that they explained clearly, when making an engagement, about " time off " and holidays allowed (though they had thought that two weeks' holiday in the year, with wages, was an understood thing) ; that wages were, of course, settled by agreement, and that it was impossible to stereotype conditions of employment further. It might perhaps be well, as one legal correspondent suggested, to have a simple form of agreement of this sort drawn up and printed (as is sometimes done in engaging agricultural labourers) so that it would be readily accessible to such employers and employees as wished for it. But if so, the agreement should deal briefly with essentials only, for experience in apprenticeship indentures has shown the difficulty of enforcing detailed conditions of service unless both employer and employed are carefully selected. The knowledge that such an agreement had been signed, even without definite legal force, might occasionally check irresponsible employers and maids from throwing up engagements just made. They would, however, be only of limited value.

The domestic worker, except in very exacting forms of service, has now established, to a great extent, the type of work that she will consent to do, though there still remain some hard-worked and adaptable servants, especially in houses containing children or invalids, who, like the mediæval villein of the law-books, " know not when they rise in the morning what they shall do in the rest of the day." The husband in the old song, who said " he could do as much work in a day as his wife could do in three," and exchanged occupations with her for the day, realised this, the eternal drawback to domestic work, only too keenly. But the modern servant and the capable mistress have, to a great extent, diminished and brought order into these varied occupations. The good housewife, who is reappearing in the world, will probably find it both possible and desirable to make her different servants' work rather more definite. Such comparative definiteness might quite fairly be asked for in return for greater efficiency.

Mistresses sent in some suggestions on this point which fall into three groups :—

    (i.) Servants, or their mothers if they are young, should ask many more (sensible) questions than they usually do when applying to an employer.

    (ii.) A servants' time-table (not too detailed) should, *if possible*, be drawn up, and adhered to.

    (iii.) Clear agreements as to hours of sleep should be made, especially with regard to young workers.

These seem useful and unassuming recommendations.

Further suggestions of a practical nature neither they, nor the servants, seemed able to produce.

(vi.) METHODS OF ORGANISATION.—As has been said in the previous section, one chief characteristic of domestic service is that the relationship of employer and employed is indefinite and unorganised. Should it be more organised in the technical sense ? And, if so, how ?

Most mistresses—fresh from recent experience of strikes —wrote virtually that such organisation was totally unnecessary, since conditions for the servant had improved steadily and were still improving, while wages were constantly rising from the relation of supply to demand ; that modern Trade Unions were of doubtful advantage at any time, especially in their effects on home life, and even if skill could be guaranteed by combination of workers, ninety-nine per cent. of mistresses would prefer " inefficient but willing blacklegs " ; while those classes of servant who really needed protection would not join a Union, and could hardly be benefited thereby. At present there are, at least, two domestic servants' Unions in existence. Further there is the Domestic Servants' Insurance Society, which, although in no sense a Trade Union, is much stronger numerically than either Union, and has great possibilities before it in giving a sense of *esprit-de-corps* to scattered servants.

Against Trade Unionism for servants there are the following points : (1) The workers are scattered and have little means of acquiring a sense of comradeship. The difficulties in organising them on a large scale would be nearly as great as those which have prevented the effective organisation of the home-worker in industry.

(2) The interests and outlook of the older and younger workers, the housekeeper and the between-maid, are apt to be totally different. The interests of the former, as their replies show, tend to approach that of the employer much more than that of the beginner.

(3) The chief drawbacks to service turn on precisely those personal and non-economic questions with which trade unionism has, as yet, not tried to deal.

(4) The difficulties in enforcing the decisions of a Domestic

Union in individual cases, even by collective bargaining, or by a strike, seem almost insuperable. Hours of work might indeed be regulated by a Trade Union, but even these must be elastic.

A well-organised Union might, on a small scale, have the advantage of consolidating a body of opinion in a definite area or class of domestic work. But domestic service is, to some extent, an anachronism. You cannot modernise industrial conditions within it unless you transform these conditions completely. It is not like other trades, because here, if you get rid of the capitalist, you get rid of the industry. Perhaps, in the future, when a race of skilled daily servants has arisen, it may be possible and desirable to standardise agreements with employers.

Is the fertility of human invention unable to suggest anything better than present-day unionism to deal with the servant questions ? A number of writers have urged the establishment of some kind of guild, or groups of guilds, which might either include employers and maids for the organisation of service in a given locality, or should consist solely of groups of maids, perhaps supplying their own utensils and guaranteeing efficiency of service. Again, it has been suggested that much good might be done by an influential local advisory committee representing different interests, which should try, merely by recommendation, to standardise good conditions for servants. Such attempts or suggestions towards trade organisation are clearly experimental and it is impossible to dogmatise on the subject yet. It seems clear that improvements in domestic service will come, if at all, partly by improved public opinion in the employing class, partly by the intelligent demands of reasonable bodies of servants, clear as to what improvements they desire and able to supply efficient service in return ; partly—but, let us hope, only in the last resort—by restrictive legislation.

PART THREE

THE INDUSTRIAL AND PERSONAL ASPECTS
MEET : SUMMARY

IN the outside world it is being realised that the payment
of wages and the performance of work do not terminate
the relationship of employer and employed. The sense of
a further responsibility is not new, but it is now steadily
making its way in industrial life. The cash nexus, pure
and simple, is peculiarly unsatisfactory in domestic service,
although there is a common tendency to rely on it, especially
in some types of large household, and among restless servants and busy or indifferent (or disillusioned) employers.
A steady country servant expressed this well :—

" It is rather difficult for me to say what improvements should
be made in service, as I have been fortunate enough to have had good
places, only having been in four during the twenty years I have been
in service, and I think very often there are faults on both sides.
Want of confidence between mistress and maid is one of the chief
causes, I often think, of servants' leaving : there should be a little
more giving and taking on both sides, and a little more faith. Some
mistresses are so ready to look on the girls as mere machines to do
their will, while the maids, on the other hand, simply think of the
lady as a Banking Account, to get all the cash they can out of, and
then go to some one else who can pay higher."

This attitude may become more common and may, with
reasonable modifications, be comparatively satisfactory
among the well-organised daily servants of the future.
But it is quite impossible to organise domestic service, as
at present understood, on the "machine and banking
account" basis ; both because servants must perforce
generally be in such specially close relation to the life of the
family for which they work, and because the large majority
of servants are so young. At the date of the census of
1911, 417,000 servants were under twenty years old, and
760,000 were under twenty-five. For these, at least, the

mistress, generally an older woman with more education and, presumably, more knowledge of the world, ought to feel personal responsibility. Even with elder servants, the need for leisure and " self-development " reappears as a necessity that no merely business arrangement can satisfy. To a certain extent, opportunities for these may be claimed as part of the implied contract of service ; but the sensible use of such opportunities cannot possibly be reduced to legal or conventional rights.

Such provision is, of course, often made with the utmost care and success by mistresses already. But there are still a great number who do not use their imagination and sympathy in this way, just as there are numbers of selfish servants who never step beyond, if they reach, what they are professionally bound to do for their pay. " I have always found that if you study a mistress, she will study you," wrote numbers of contented servants. This represents the "give-and-take" relationship crudely, but on the whole, satisfactorily.

Are the moral dangers of service greater than in other callings normally open to girls ? This was made a special question to employers, and was answered thoughtfully and in very different ways. About equal numbers answered respectively, that temptations in service were greater, or less, than those in shop or factory or office work. The fact remains that a very large number of cases in rescue-homes are drawn from domestic service. But this, in itself, proves little, for apart from the fact that the girl who is or has been in service is probably more readily helped in trouble by the outside worker, a very large proportion of these servants are almost defective and not of the type that often obtains factory or shop work. Recent legislation will, though only to a certain extent, deal with such cases.[1]

The difference in types of service once more makes it

[1] Some useful suggestions were made as to the position of the feeble-minded in service. A large number of correspondents wrote, " keep them out of service." A number of others with definite experience wrote, " let the feeble-minded—if reasonably fit—go into service," but only under inspection with specially selected mistresses, and without other servants, unless these are much older. Often the slightly feeble-minded spend happy and quite useful lives in service, and experience shows that kind mistresses can be found who will look after them.

practically impossible to generalise about such individual
temptations. There are special dangers in some large,
ill-regulated households, which arise partly from the
presence of men and women servants, with betting and
other lures brought closely to them, but difficulties are
probably most often to be found in the small, single-
servant situations, where, despite all the efforts of Girls'
Friendly Society, Young Women's Christian Association,
Metropolitan Association for Befriending Young Servants,
etc., it is hard altogether to safeguard the young worker
from the temptations of evenings out and from employers'
neglect. The following quotation from a long and sensibly
worded letter sent by a North-country general servant
illustrates an extreme form of such callousness.

" A young girl where I live was locked out all night because she
was a few minutes late, and the neighbours heard her ring and ring
again, but her mistress refused to come down, and the poor girl
spent the night in an out-house on the clay floor."

In no direction is the lack of common-sense, to put it on
the lowest grounds, shown more disastrously both among
employers of girls and parents.

Other special temptations alluded to in the replies received
were the evils of the hire purchase system and the system of
secret commissions among servants. Some correspondents
suggested that both of these should be prohibited, but it
was generally felt on consideration that fresh grandmotherly
legislation for servants as such was not wanted, though
hire purchase in any case might be wisely prohibited for
minors. The difference of age and class is the constant
drawback to all rigid legal restrictions with regard to
servants, a number of whom are really only silly children
in mind and years, often with equally irresponsible and
uncomprehending employers. This is one of the good
reasons why the work of bringing together mistresses and
young maids should be taken over by the Labour Exchanges
as representing an impartial outside authority ; for the
education of opinion about conditions of service is
very important, both in the employing and employed
class.

There is no one panacea for the difficulties of domestic
service, and the following conclusions, drawn from the

G

material collected above, must therefore seem rather indefinite.

The servant problem is (a) personal, (b) industrial. The two aspects are interdependent. The importance of the first makes it impossible to treat domestic service at present like other trades.

(a) The replies showed a frequent sense of deprivation among servants as a result of their calling—a loss of liberty, of interests, of companionship or of caste, as compared with other workers. A good deal of this is wholly unreasonable, but it clearly exists, and is important. The remedy must be largely personal, i.e., through the exercise of imagination and sympathy on the part of the employer (especially of young servants) and of the employed.

(b) (i.) The servants and employers consulted agreed as a whole that improved accommodation should be further considered, especially in the building of new houses.

(ii.) There seemed to be an almost universal desire for more definite hours, with a limited provision of daily time off, and more access to fresh air. This in itself would solve many of the difficulties of lack of interests, companionship and liberty.

(iii.) Few grievances seemed to be felt as to wages or uniforms, though a few useful suggestions were made on these points.

(iv.) The " prospects " of service as compared with other forms of wage-earning were held to be good for the capable servant while so occupied, good for her home after marriage, but only moderately good for the worker, who, after marriage or widowhood, had to become self-supporting again.

(v.) A great desire was shown, especially among employers, to improve conditions of entry, and to establish a standard of efficiency quite as much among employers as among maids.

(vi.) Considerable distrust was shown as to registries—especially as to those of small and moderate size—and a rather doubtful confidence in the competence of Labour Exchanges to deal with the work. As a whole, more hope seemed to be felt in advertisement as a means of effecting engagements.

(vii.) Much disapproval was expressed on all sides concerning the system of servants' references, as being one-sided and inadequate ; but the difficulty of sweeping reforms was felt to be great. The Irish system of written statements from the mistress in every situation was approved, as was also the development of the system of obtaining mistresses' references for young workers.

(viii.) A small number only of servants and mistresses expressed a desire for social clubs or trade unionism for servants. The mistresses appeared to be more hopeful about clubs than the servants.

It seems probable that the whole organisation of domestic service will in due course be transformed as it is brought more into line with other forms of women's employment. But during the period of transition there will be ample room for effort and experiment in improving methods of training and in establishing some recognised standard of efficiency, while the unnecessary drudgery of domestic work is lightened ; in securing more liberty in the best sense of the term for the domestic worker, and in raising the conditions of service to those which already exist between the best employers and maids.

AN EMPLOYER'S CONCLUSIONS

By Lady Willoughby de Broke

In accepting the invitation of the Women's Industrial Council to write a short chapter upon the thorny question of Domestic Service, in connection with their recent very interesting enquiry into its attendant drawbacks or advantages, I will deal only with the pre-War period. The last eighteen months have brought about such an upheaval of our home-life and customs, and these are at present in such a fluid state, that it would be waste of time to attempt to deal with the situation as it is now, or as it may be after the War. The demand for women as munition-workers and the many other doors that have been opened to them, have caused many to abandon Domestic Service for the greater liberty and apparent higher pay to be obtained elsewhere ; I say apparent because Domestic Service has the advantage of being one of the few wage-earning occupations where the rise in food prices and higher taxation remains unfelt. At present it is impossible to foretell how our social life will readjust itself when we revert to normal conditions, therefore let us confine ourselves to the period preceding August, 1914, and look into the conditions then prevailing. In writing on this complex question I wish to disclaim any intention of " laying down the law." The views I put forward have been formed as a result of twenty-five years' experience in managing households varying in size from some twenty servants down to a small ménage of four only. I can truthfully say that during that time very few so-called " servant troubles " have arisen and that I have received the most devoted service from many. I have discussed the subject with a very large number of employers and employees and endeavoured to ascertain where the shoe pinches and what measures servants them-

100

selves would wish to see adopted in order to remove
hardships.

For many years past there has been a growing prejudice
against Domestic Service, and enquiry into the causes will
assuredly be welcomed by all good employers with a view to
grievances being brought to light and remedied. Many of
these grievances appear perfectly legitimate and I will deal
briefly with the principal ones.

Servants have great difficulty in finding out anything
definite about their prospective employer or situation before-
hand. If they unwittingly enter into an undesirable,
possibly even not a respectable household, they may forfeit
their previous good character, because employers often
object to furnishing a second reference and a servant's good
name is easily tarnished by service in a bad household.
Registry offices are much better managed nowadays, but
they should endeavour to obtain more information about
the general character of a household before recommending
a servant to apply there. The trouble is that the employers
with whom the Registry Offices are most constantly in touch
are obviously those who do not keep their servants long
and presumably have not the best households. The really
good employer comparatively seldom needs to apply to a
Registry. If a vacancy is likely to occur, an application
is often received privately from some servant in the neighbourhood, or from a relative or friend of an employee about
the place. The same applies to the good servant. He or
she will usually get passed on from one household to another
with a warm recommendation and thus there will be no
need of Registry Offices in such cases. There is a curious
prejudice against allowing a servant to see a situation before
engagement. Surely it would be well that she should see
the household and her future fellow-servants, thus enabling
her to form some opinion as to whether she is likely to settle
down happily among them. When one considers the lack
of privacy and constant enforced companionship of a
heterogeneous staff, it is a marvel that they get on as well
together as they usually do. In any case the fullest questions
should be asked and answered on either side before an
agreement is reached. Here undoubtedly the employer is
at an advantage as she can obtain a reference about the

servant, but too much importance should not be attached to references. Employers complain of the difficulty of getting truthful characters of servants from their previous situations. Sometimes grave faults are glossed over or evaded ; on the other hand, if a servant gives notice, ladies are apt to exaggerate small failings and so prevent the servant from obtaining another place. In my own experience I have found it advisable to pay but little heed to references which may not be quite satisfactory. There is no perfection in this world and the servant who is dubbed " unwilling " or " unsatisfactory " in one situation, can often be transformed into a good worker by a little kindness and firmness. So much depends upon the employer. A good mistress makes a good servant. This is proved by the fact that certain employers always have good servants who stay with them for years while others can never keep their staff. The latter soon become known among servants and they find great difficulty in getting anyone to serve them even through they may offer high wages and " liberal outings." Indeed some servants look askance at such offers, as they at once infer that the situation is undesirable, else baits of that kind would be unnecessary.

In this country we suffer greatly from the lack of domestic training among all classes. Household work and management should be taught to all girls, no matter what their social status may be, and the inefficiency of the employer is often the cause of inefficiency in the servant. For this reason it is an immense advantage to a servant to begin at the bottom of the ladder in a large household, where she will learn her duties under skilled supervision. In the small one or two-servant households where there is no one but the mistress to supervise, there appears frequently to be no method or system of work at all. The mistress has usually never been taught and therefore cannot herself teach the proper organization of duties, and her servants have little chance of becoming efficient. After years in such service they often do not know how to clean plate or make a bed properly.

I would urge ladies, who are in a position to do so, to take young girls more frequently into their houses and train them. They learn more quickly and become far more efficient when accustomed early to the routine of a well-organized establishment than if they drift into the post of " general " in a small house where they pick up their duties mainly by the light of nature, and have little hope of rising to superior positions in the future. Ladies would be doing a great national work if they would train girls in larger numbers, and such training appears for some reason more successful than that given in Industrial Institutions, Schools of Domestic Economy, or other public organizations, and it is astonishing how rapidly an under-sized girl grows and develops when well-fed and looked after in a good house. A well-trained domestic servant is of real value to the nation, she makes the best possible wife and mother, as she has acquired a good knowledge of house-wifery and habits of cleanliness, punctuality, and, to some extent, of hygiene. There are few cottage homes where the wife has previously been in good service that are not models of neatness and comfort. If for some reason, such as the husband's ill-health or death, she is obliged to return to wage-earning at any time, she can always find a means of livelihood and is much sought after by employers to take an odd job, do sewing, washing, or go out cooking or charing.

The idea that domestic servants are at a disadvantage in regard to opportunities for marriage is, I think, exaggerated. There are few girls of average appearence, who have not got a " young man," but the rule rigidly enfored in many houses of " no followers," appears to be barbarous and inhuman, besides being dangerous. Young people will contrive to meet somehow and it would be far better for the mistress to gain the girl's confidence and, if the young man is respectable and worthy of her, to allow them to meet openly and frankly at suitable times and places. The endeavour to suppress what is a perfectly natural desire for companionship can only lead to surreptitious meetings after dark and very likely to grave trouble. If the girl is very young and has no mother near by, much good might be done by the mistress giving her a little friendly warning and advice about the great physical laws of life and birth.

A servant's existence, especially where only one or two are kept, is often necessarily a lonely one, and although

" outings " are more liberal nowadays, there is still room for improvement in that respect. In towns well-conducted clubs where servants could meet their friends when off duty might be of great benefit, but in country districts they would be impracticable. Much more might however be done in allowing servants to invite a friend to tea occasionally, also a visit to a theatre or local entertainment would greatly help to break the somewhat cruel monotony of many servants' lives. It is rather sad that a girl should ask in trepidation whether she will be allowed to bring her bicycle to a new situation. Fortunately such unreasonable prejudices are dying out and many girls now have the possibility of this healthy exercise and refreshment. They should, however, be encouraged, whenever the work permits, to go out in the daylight and not after dark as is often the case ; especially should this rule apply to young girls unless they are accompanied by some responsible person.

Hard and fast rules as regards hours off duty are not popular among servants. So much depends on circumstances and a good deal of elasticity will be found to work best.   If it should be a wet day an outing is of no use and should be transferable. If there are guests in the house and extra work to be done, no outings may be possible at all. If on the other hand the employers are away, the servants should be encouraged to go out as much as possible. If liberty is allowed in choosing their own times to suit the general welfare of the household, and confidence is placed in them in these matters, the majority will not abuse it.

Fortunately the custom of allowing an annual holiday with wages is growing rapidly and at least a fortnight should be the minimum. In small households this may be very inconvenient, but the mistress or daughter of the house should be prepared to act as substitute unless outside help can be afforded.

There are two grievances specially appertaining to large households to which I would like to call attention. When parties are given, dinner is often very late and servants don't get supper till 10.30 or 11 p.m. and consequently cannot go to bed till all hours. Some plan might surely be devised to enable servants to sup earlier. A cold snack would satisfy many in emergency if only they could get it, but there is so much red-tape in big houses that they cannot obtain a crust of bread out of meal time. Too much is left to the cook or housekeeper, and upon her or him depends the comfort of the others. More especially where a chef is kept the servants' meals are often very badly cooked by an inexperienced under-kitchenmaid and good food ruined. In such houses the late hours are very trying to the staff. It is unreasonable to expect servants to stay up till 12 or 1 a.m. in order to turn out the lights and then to be down early next morning. The plan of keeping the maid up to unfasten her lady's gown on her return from parties and balls, possibly several times a week in the London season, is thoughtless and selfish. A little trouble will easily enable us to do this for ourselves.

The question of accommodation for servants has greatly improved since the days of dark basements and the herding together of several in one room. There is still scope for improvement however in this respect, more especially in old-fashioned London houses, where the servants' quarters are sometimes disgraceful in their darkness, lack of ventilation, and sanitary conveniences. I would, however, like to register an emphatic protest against any scheme for encouraging daily service and hostels of residence. This would open the door to much trouble and danger, especially in the case of young girls. Servants who have discussed this proposition with me speak very strongly in disapproval. What possible protection can be extended to a girl leaving her employer's house after dark, to go to a hostel or even to return to her own home ? Neither her employer nor her relatives know how long she spends en route, nor what acquaintances she may pick up. Apart from this grave danger, it entails earlier rising and in bad weather it would mean great hardship. If the girl were ill in a hostel, who would look after her ? The system would also in my opinion tend to less close mutual interests between mistress and maid. It is the lack of this which is at the bottom of most of our servant troubles. Do not let us encourage anything which may loosen the tie between them.

The desire which some servants feel for a frequent " change " is greatly to be deplored. I have even been told that there is some kind of Union to which footmen belong which forbids their remaining over two years in any situation. While fully realising that under servants have every right to wish to rise in their profession, there are often opportunities that will enable them by exercising a little patience to get advancement in the household where they are ; again, if they show ability, a just mistress will herself help a servant on to a better position.   In any case when a servant has risen to a head post in a good situation, let nothing but marriage or grave private reasons cause her to seek a change.   Long service in one family leads to mutual respect and affection.   When age or failing health compel a dissolution of such a bond, a pension and often a legacy are very properly forthcoming, but compulsion in this matter might do much harm.

Definite contracts, trade organizations and guarantees of efficiency are all in my opinion undesirable, and the latter at least impracticable as well.   Domestic Service is of all others the most difficult in which to define efficiency. One style of cookery suits one person which is repugnant to another.   In one house a footman is selected for his height and appearance, in another a good worker irrespective of looks is desired.   It would press very hardly on the elderly servant who (apart from this war time) has already sufficient difficulty with the absurd " too old at forty " idea and is reduced to hair-dyeing and prevarication in order to get a job.   What is to happen to the worthy man-servant of 55 who, though grown somewhat slow and a trifle deaf, is quite well suited to a quiet country situation ? Is he " efficient " ?

The National Insurance Act has been a distinct boon in the case of Domestic Service, so far as my experiences go, more especially for those who belong to the really admirable Domestic Servants Insurance Society, which now provides for dental treatment in addition to their other benefits.

Personal saving is more common than most people think. Servants are wonderfully generous in helping to support relatives, but in spite of this, most steady servants put by a a little annually.   It is true that many men-servants unfortunately squander their money in betting, but there again we ought to help them by advice and still more by example to refrain from such follies.

The question of raising the status of Domestic Service is a very difficult one, as indeed is the whole problem of class distinction. It appears universal in all walks of life and curiously enough exists in quite as sharp lines among servants as elsewhere. It is true that the tradespeople at a village dance will hold aloof from the servants present, but the cook would be considered equally to lose caste were she to go for a walk with the second footman or were the lady's maid to be friends with the third housemaid. Indeed class prejudice among servants themselves is most difficult to combat, upper servants not caring to associate with the relatives or friends of the under servants and being inclined to boycott them when they are invited to tea.

Official titles would I believe be very unpopular. In certain houses it is the custom to address the cook as "cook," but this does not raise her in her profession, it lowers her, and such a title would greatly offend a cook of higher grade, who is always addressed as Mrs. So and So as a courtesy title, whether married or single. Indeed upper servants are invariably called by their surname with the prefix of Mr., Mrs. or Miss in the household, and every servant has the chance of rising to this position if efficient. Under servants only are called by their Christian names and I have never heard of any objection being raised to this custom.

Having now dealt with the main points which are apt to cause trouble and friction in the household, I would urge with all the power at my command the necessity for fostering a more intimate and human relationship between employer and employed as being the only real solution of the difficulty. By all means let us do all we can to educate the public to consider Domestic Service the highly honourable trade which indeed it is. But we want more than that. The ideal mistress should look upon herself as a sort of foster-mother to the servants and more especially in the case of young girls who are inmates of her house. It is a great responsibility and there is such a splendid opportunity for a really wise and sympathetic woman to guide and influence for good those who are under her roof. Small households are easier to deal with in this respect. In large ones the housekeeper often stands in the way.

Servants are so quick to respond to a kind word or a

little friendly interest.   They will often say that they don't mind what they do or how hard they work if only they are treated as human beings and not as machines by their employers.   When we consider how wonderfully responsive servants are to our joys and sorrows, and how they will toil to ensure the success of a ball or of a wedding party, and how willingly they will take on extra duties in the event of illness in the house, we might easily extend a little more sympathy to them and their affairs.

Above all let us not mistrust our servants.   They are very quick to perceive any tendency to suspicion and nothing so rouses their resentment.   When we think of the amazing trust that perforce we repose in them and how seldom it is abused, we must admit that servants as a class are wonderfully honest.   We entrust our jewels and laces to the maid and our wines and valuable plate to the butler with a confidence that is rarely misplaced.   Those houses where nothing is kept locked away from the servants are I fancy the most secure of all.

Let us live simply ourselves, not loading our tables with expensive luxuries while we expect our servants to live on cold mutton.   The War has shown us how ready they are to make sacrifices in food, firing and such like economies. This cheerful spirit and willingness to " do their bit " must not be forgotten, though I must not enter on it at greater length now.

Employers hold the future of Domestic Service mainly in their own hands.   Let us all do our share in uplifting it and establishing it as an honourable and desirable profession on the high plane where it deserves to be.

APPENDIX I

EXISTING MEANS OF TRAINING GIRLS FOR DOMESTIC
SERVICE

Before sketching the present heterogeneous provision of domestic
teaching, two points must be emphasised; first that it is impossible to distinguish completely between training for domestic
service, and training which aims at preparing a girl to manage a
working-class home, since the ground-work of both must be the
same ; and second that any good education which develops common-
sense and resourcefulness is nearly as good a preparation for the
less specialised forms of domestic service as is definite trade training.
Since, however, the elementary schools as a whole emphatically do
not unaided prepare girls either to manage a house satisfactorily or
to meet readily all the varied demands of domestic service, there is
clearly need for more training.   At present this is given as follows :—

In the girls' own homes.—This, at its best, is still the most
satisfactory preparation for either form of domestic work.   A
number of the servants circularised by the Women's Industrial
Council replied to this effect to the question, " What training had
you before going into service ? "   " Only from my mother ; I had
the best of mothers, and she taught me all I needed to know before
I went out at sixteen."   But the number of mothers competent to
give such home training to their daughters is limited, and seems
likely to lessen.

At the elementary schools.—Definite training in certain domestic
subjects is now given to all girl pupils above the infants' classes in
State schools.   These are summarised in the Board of Education's
Code of Regulations for Public Elementary Schools in England
(1912), p. 3.

" *Domestic subjects* (for girls only) including the proper performance of ordinary domestic duties, together with instruction in
needlework and knitting.   The older girls should receive a practical
training in cookery, laundry-work and housewifery, except where
circumstances render this impossible." . . .

(a) " Needlework should be so taught as to secure a practical
knowledge of sewing, cutting-out and making ordinary garments,
together with mending and darning.   Exercises on small pieces of
material should be used only for learning different kinds of stitches.
In all classes the periodical construction and completion of some
useful garment by each scholar should be aimed at, and the older
girls may be taught the use and care of the sewing machine with
advantage.   At the same time the educational value of needlework

as a form of hand and eye training must be kept in view as well as
its practical value." This is the basis of the definite change in the
teaching of sewing which has taken place recently in elementary
schools. The *chef d'œuvre* produced by many months' labour is
now becoming a thing of the past ; instead, quite little girls practise
on trousseaux for their own and other people's dolls, mend their
small sisters' torn clothes (if their mothers can be induced to let them
bring these to school), and progress gradually till at fourteen they
cut out and make outfits for themselves or for the life-size doll on
which the top class at school often practises child-nursing. All
this means much more work for the teachers than did the older,
uniform system ; and the degree to which it can really be fresh and
elastic depends greatly on individual teachers and the size of the
school. Cheap, ready-made clothes and long hours of work are
unfortunately great deterrents to home needlework after a girl has
left school.

(b) *Cookery.*—This, when well taught, is probably one of the
favourite subjects at school, since it is taken just at the age—twelve
or thirteen years old—when an active girl is apt to look forward to
her future work when she will have left school, and to long for
something practical. In 1911-12 courses of cookery lessons consisting of not less than forty hours were attended by 245,000 girls
out of a total of 505,000 between twelve and fifteen on the elementary
school attendance roll in England. The instruction is generally
given in a specially equipped cookery centre, to which successive
pupils from neighbouring schools are drafted. The expense of the
equipment and the cost of material are an obvious difficulty, especially in poor urban districts and in the country, though the children
are encouraged to buy their own productions and the food prepared
at the cookery classes is sometimes eaten at the dining centres for
underfed school children. Many ingenious experiments have been
tried by local education authorities for the benefit of rural districts.
The county authorities of Radnor, Gloucestershire and Yorkshire
have provided cookery vans, which tour about the county with halts
of from two to three weeks in different villages. To these, girls of
from ten and a half upwards are sent from neighbouring schools for
brief periods of instruction. In other places the clergyman's wife
or the schoolmistress has offered up her kitchen and range for a few
little girls' instruction. But in such cases there are difficulties in
getting technically qualified teachers, a necessity for earning the
Government grant which keeps down the rates. The examples
quoted below of Lindsey and Hampshire illustrate more comprehensive ways of dealing with the problem. Derbyshire recently
tried to meet the difficulty by " specially training certain selected
persons resident in the more remote parts of the area, in order that
they might teach cookery in their own villages." The teaching
given by these persons " has been attended with marked success."

(c) *Laundrywork.*—This has been taught definitely as a school
subject since 1905. It has not been so popular as cookery, and is
taken by fewer schools, partly, again, owing to the cost of equip-

ment and the small number of pupils who can be taught at once. It is, however, being more widely learnt. In 1911-12 grants were earned for courses of twenty lessons by 94,000, and for longer courses by 20,000 pupils. The Board of Education encourages its adoption by decreeing that no one shall proceed to the popular classes in combined domestic subjects until after some laundry lessons.

(d) *Hygiene.*—This includes instruction in the elementary rules of personal health, particularly in respect of food, drink, clothing, cleanliness and fresh air, but this subject may be extended and interpreted by the teacher into meaning almost anything connected with the management of a house, an invalid, or a baby. It is naturally apt to suffer from being treated too theoretically.

(e) A new subject has been creeping recently into school timetables, under the official title of combined domestic subjects, or more euphemistically, home-making. This may take different forms ; but it generally means that the pupils work in small numbers either in a centre fitted up with two or three rooms, or in a house occupied by some of the teachers, who are waited on and sleep in beds made by successive thirteen-year-olds, or in a small tenement cottage rented or bought for the purpose. We give a few examples from centres, under the management of enlightened local authorities : (i.) Chester ; (ii.) Lindsey ; (iii.) Bristol ; (iv.) Hampshire.

(i.) CHESTER

CITY AND COUNTY OF THE CITY OF CHESTER EDUCATION COMMITTEE.

The children attend every day for a full month, staying till the end of the afternoon.

They are taught to go to market and spend their money properly, to arrange and cook their own dinners. (They may eat them afterwards on payment of 1d.)

Four teachers live at this cottage centre. 150 girls attend the cottage centre annually.

(ii.) LINDSEY

In May, 1910, an attempt was made to give a practical bias to school work in certain selected rural schools. This experiment has succeeded so well that it has been extended, and has been followed with modifications in the County of Nottingham. We may quote from a report of H.M. Inspectors in May, 1914 : " Under former conditions . . . on an average two-and-a-half to three hours per week were given to manual occupations. . . . Now seven-and-a-half hours (or between a quarter and a third of the total time given to secular instruction) is devoted to handwork, etc. . . . The children are very keen, and handwork has obviously made school life more attractive. . . . This is especially the case in certain instances of dull children, whose interest in their other work and general belief in themselves was much increased by the discovery that they could at least hold their own in handwork. . . . In schools where it is introduced, domestic work seems to be the branch arousing most interest, and there was much evidence brought forward that country parents find it most useful." A few of the small country schools, to which the experiment refers, have been provided with special rooms for their practical work. In most cases the work—cookery or laundry—has to be done at one end of a class-room, or in the teacher's own house. Such teaching must at present be somewhat informal, but the inspection report shows that it is well worth while to continue and develop it.

(iii.) Bristol Education Committee

Home Management Scheme

Twelve girls who have had previous instruction in Cookery and Laundrywork attend daily for seven weeks, entirely carrying out the work of a six-roomed house in which three people reside.

Mornings.	Group 1 : *Cookery.*	Group 2 : *Laundry-work.*	Group 3 : *House-wifery.*
	(4 Girls).	(4 Girls).	(4 Girls).
9–9.45.	9.45–12 noon.	9.45–12 noon.	9.45–12 noon.
Monday—	Cooking dinner.	Monday—Mending,	*Weekly* care of a room.
Meals planned.	Making all Bread,	sorting, steeping	Two girls will turn out
Tuesday—	Cakes, etc. required	clothes.	and clean one room.
Work of house	by household.	Tuesday—Washing	daily.
planned.	Preparing for tea	clothes.	*Daily care.*
Wednesday—	and supper.	Wednesday—Ironing,	Steps and brass.
Thursday—	All utensils to be	airing, etc.	Bedrooms.
Shopping done.	cleaned and put	Thursday—Cleaning	Sitting-room.
Friday—	away after using.	woodwork in class-room and kitchen.	Passage and lava-tory.
		Friday—Cleaning	Laying table.
		flues and all tins,	Keeping accounts.
		brass, silver and	One girl to act as
		kitchen utensils.	housekeeper and
		(These girls will	keep accounts of
		carry out usual	weekly expendi-
		kitchenmaid's duties	ture.
		throughout the week.)	
Afternoons.	2–2.30 p.m.	2.30–4 p.m.	2–4.30.
Monday—		Theory Lessons from	Laying tea-table and
Tuesday—	Washing up and	approved House-	preparing supper
Wednesday—	clearing kitchen.	wifery Syllabus,	tray.
Thursday—		varied with practice	
Friday—		in renovations and	
		lessons on re-making	
		garments and use of	
		sewing-machine.	

Each group consists of four girls who exchange duties with another group at end of week ; thus in six weeks each girl will have had the same duties twice ; the last week will be devoted to revision and special instruction in care of infants.

"We have two centres, and they are proving very successful. The dinners are prepared and served by the children, who are taught to observe good behaviour at the table."

(iv.) Hampshire

"There is a staff working in the county of some twelve teachers, each as near as possible fixed in a centre from which a portion of the county is worked. The principal work is giving instruction in cook-ery and in a few cases laundrywork ; this instruction is given in elementary schools or evening schools, but whatever the arrangement is, they give ten lessons a week.   In addition there is a travelling Housewifery School that is presided over by a trained teacher who is called a Housemother, and the purpose is to reach remote rural centres that could not be touched by the resident staff.   We get either a village hall or a cottage and set up housekeeping for the girls over eleven years of age from the elementary school.   Sometimes, if a school is a very small one, we try to arrange for girls to come from two neighbouring schools, in which case the cottage has to be found somewhere conveniently situated between the two positions.   The instruction is given for one complete month during which the girls do not go into the elementary school at all.   They come to the cottage at nine in the morning, and leave it at four o'clock in the afternoon, and the work is very thoroughly done. There is probably no part of the domestic work that has given greater satisfaction or done more good in the county.   It has brought the mothers into touch with it, and the girls, having regard to the comparatively short time they are under instruction, become fairly efficient.   They have to do housework, cooking, laundrywork, mending and darning, in addition to any small household accounts which have to be kept, and it appears from reports received that the girls return to the school all the better for this month at the cottage centre.   It has brought them into touch with the actualities of life. The arithmetic they do relates to real things, and their writing has not suffered, because they have to write out the recipes and keep their notebooks up to date ; even reading is not overlooked, because occasionally while some girls are at work one of the number will read a story."

These courses may make, in the opinion of some, a regrettable break in the well-planned school curriculum for the older girls, and to a certain extent they remove the pupils from the head teacher's influence.   If, however, the classes are well managed, their attraction and value are great.   At thirteen no normal child is insusceptible to the glamour of keeping house, of going to market and finding the use of the detached lessons in cookery previously received. Any type of girl may obviously gain greatly from this sort of work, especially from its educational value in linking theory to practice. But its utilitarian value is greatest in the very poor neighbourhoods, where a standard is sorely needed, not necessarily for domestic service, but for " home-making " in its most literal sense.   The structural expense sometimes involved and the provision of special teachers are drawbacks which deter many educational authorities from providing such teaching.   It is, however, greatly to be hoped that it may be extended and that some of the present restrictions on its introduction may be relaxed.

In 1911-12, 7,000 girls earned grants of 10s. a head for, at least, eighty hours' instruction in combined domestic subjects, while 28,000 earned grants in housewifery, generally for twenty hour courses.

The last general report on teaching of domestic subjects to public elementary school children (1912) expressed satisfaction at the increased quantity and quality of such teaching. Though some local authorities are very slow in making adequate provision, and though the ideal of bringing instruction in domestic subjects within reach of every girl attending such schools is still far from being realised, yet much progress is being made. Also the instruction given is of a much more practical nature than in the past, and more care is taken to bring the work into close connection with the circumstances of the children's homes. Much, however, remains to be done in this latter respect.

TRAINING AFTER THE COMPULSORY SCHOOL AGE.—A very large variety of expedients exist.

(1) *Day training courses.*

(a) " Home-making centres."

These are new phenomena. They correspond to the " centres " previously described for children attending the elementary schools, though their scope is wider. Thus Brighton has a Municipal School for Home Training which admits forty girls, who attend, if possible, " straight from the elementary school " from 9 to 4.30 on five days a week for a term of twenty-one weeks, at a fee of sixpence a week. "The lessons learned in class are at once put into practice by the pupils actually doing the whole of the daily work of school and house ; while one group cooks the school dinner, another is working in the laundry or sewing-room, and each group in turn gets six weeks' practical experience of complete housekeeping in the model home, consisting of sitting-room, bedrooms, kitchen and bath-room, used as a residence by three mistresses. The aim of the school is that girls should realise the value and interest of all home-making work, so that no household task may be regarded as drudgery." In a recent report of the Juvenile Employment Sub-committee it is mentioned that the girls so trained are specially sought after by mistresses, though their training is as much for home as for " service." Liverpool has a similar fifteen weeks' course (which may be extended to thirty weeks) for girls fresh from the elementary schools. The fee for one such course is £1, but " most of the girls come with free admissions given by the Education Authority. The training is primarily for home life and not for domestic service, but we can always find places for girls who choose to go to service." Glasgow also sends a number of free pupils for such a course at the Logan and Johnston Schools of Domestic Economy, about fifty per cent. of whose pupils go into service.

Such courses are obviously most desirable. It is difficult, however, to make them quite fit the desires of the girl who most needs them, the girl from a very poor home, to whose parents the postponement of wage earning, even for a few weeks, means a definite sacrifice, while she herself is apt to feel that it places a stigma on her as compared with her late schoolfellows rejoicing in an income of five shillings a week. This has caused the failure of several well-planned schemes for such courses of training. It ought not, however, to represent a permanent barrier.

(b) Domestic training, such as is given in various London poly-technics. Their pupils do not often go into domestic service, but the training that they receive in cooking, housewifery, etc., must be a most valuable preliminary, either for home life or for the learning of dressmaking and other trade subjects.

"This school is for Junior Domestic Economy Scholars of the London County Council, and . . . their regulations state that the scholarships are given with a view to improving the standard of home life, and *not* with the idea of training for service. In point of fact a fair proportion of the girls enter service on leaving school at the end of their year's course, but the majority go into some kind of business.

" Our girls get both theoretical and practical training in house-work, cookery, needlework, dressmaking and laundry work, and a certain amount of time is given each week to English, which includes literature and composition.

" We try, in the time at our disposal, to awaken in the girls a sense of responsibility, and to rouse a real and intelligent interest in all matters pertaining to domestic work. Their compositions are written on various topics ; the books they have been reading, some question of household management or household economy, some point connected with their hygiene lessons, or occasionally a biographical or historical subject is given."

(c) Domestic training of the trade school type and standard, but definitely in preparation for the better forms of domestic service. The two London foundations of Sir John Cass and the Newcomen school have quite recently begun to give such training, helped by London County Council grants. The former takes about thirty girls at a time for a one year's course, with a second year possible ; the latter has a two years' course. Both are primarily for day scholars, but arrange for a brief period of residential training for each pupil during her course.

(d) An interesting experiment has lately been tried at Birming-ham. " Quite recently the committee opened a Day Nursery and Training School for Nursery Maids. In this about eight or ten girls attend at one time for a training of from four to six months, or, if possible, a year. The work here is carried on by a fully trained lady superintendent, and an assistant matron. Children may be left by their mothers in the Day Nursery at this school. The girls receive instruction in the actual care of babies and young children, under the direction of the lady superintendent ; also they are instructed in housework, laundrywork, cookery and the making and mending of children's clothes under the direction of the assist-ant matron. This school is, of course, for older girls, over fourteen years of age, who have left the day school and are training for a specialised form of domestic work."

(2) *Residential training.*

(a) Paid for from public funds by local education authorities.

A number of county education committees now either provide

or subsidise residential schools to which girls may go for brief courses in preparation for home life or for domestic service—almost the only way in which a country girl can earn her living. Thus the Kent education committee has a training school at Bromley, with thirty free places for young scholarship holders, who attend for a forty-two weeks' course; the Somerset education committee similarly pays for training (forty-five weeks at a time) for girls from the elementary schools, at the Glastonbury school. East Sussex has a county school at Lewes with a twenty-two weeks' course. Wiltshire sends a large number of County Council scholars to the Wiltshire School of Cookery at Trowbridge. The whole, or the greater part, of the cost is paid in these cases from the rates and taxes.

(b) Training given in reformatories, industrial schools, poor-law schools. (Sixteen certified reformatory schools for girls and one hundred and forty-six industrial schools are reported in a recent classified list.) Almost all these give domestic training, and endeavour to place their girls in service. Here again the cost is borne almost entirely from public funds, though the girls' relatives may contribute very small sums. The value of the training so given varies enormously.

(c) *Voluntary training homes.* These it is very difficult to classify, because their objects are as a rule not primarily industrial.

(i.) There is a type of voluntary home or school, which does indeed exist for domestic instruction, which admits girls only with very good references and sends them, after two or three years' skilled training, into well-paid places in service. Some Girls' Friendly Society's lodges now aim at this, though with shorter periods of training, and have introduced a special examination and certificate for which the girls in their training prepare. Excellent work of this sort has been done in the past. The chief difficulty now is the old trouble of the voluntary institution, that of getting enough funds to pay a really skilled and up-to-date staff of teachers.

The nursery training school of the Women's Industrial Council is at present unique, but comes more nearly under this heading than any other. It was established in 1912 as an experiment in the opening-up of another field of skilled employment for " working-class " girls. Girls of the elementary school type are taken at a cost of £40 for a year's residential training as nursery nurses. They are not admitted under sixteen years of age; they have a full and varied training and readily obtain good posts on leaving.

(ii.) There is the very much larger type of orphanages and " preventive " homes, of which some 240 are recorded in the returns of the reformatory and refuge union of child saving societies. One hundred and seventy of these are " institutions certified by the Poor-law Board and the Local Government Board under 25 and 26 Vict. cap. 43." These vary in training capacity from ten or twelve to the great institutions which take in two or three hundred at once. As a rule all are struggling for lack of funds, are carried on with the help of an enthusiastic underpaid or unpaid staff, and do

wonderfully good and patient work with most unpromising material.
Their successes, as recorded in their annual reports, are naturally
more often " personal " than " industrial." Few homes will admit
a girl for training at a cost of less than 5s. a week, and for less than
a year at a time. All agree that there is very little difficulty in
finding places for their girls when trained or even partially trained,
and almost all have a good opinion of the prospects offered to a girl
in service. Most make a point of keeping in touch with their former
members for some years after their first start as independent wage
earners. Some still exist which were founded in the eighteenth
century ; a much larger number date from the middle of the nine-
teenth century. Their power of adapting themselves to the needs
of the modern girl seems to vary surprisingly.

(iii.) There are also the rescue homes, and those for feeble-
minded girls—both of which often teach domestic work as a wholesome occupation, while they may or may not launch some of their
inmates into service. It is not apparently difficult to do this,
owing to the shortage of servants.

(3) *Continuation Classes.*

The great majority of the urban education authorities of the
country provide evening continuation classes in domestic subjects
for girls over fourteen. In theory these supply nearly all that is
necessary to enable a sixteen-year-old day girl to qualify for a good
situation in service. But they are not well attended, owing to the
same difficulties of very long hours of work, with the counter-
attractions and lack of industrial ambition which militate against
the success of all evening continuation classes at present.

The London County Council and other education authorities
have for some years offered scholarships by which women and girls
already in service may have half or quarter time instruction in
cookery, with maintenance grants during training.

Thus there is already a very wide provision for training in domestic
subjects. From the point of view of domestic service the main
difficulties seem to be as follows :—

(a) Girls from well-paid artisan homes who would often gladly
go in for a period of domestic training after leaving the day school
rarely at present wish to enter domestic service.

(b) Girls from poor homes, to whom the comfort and changed
surroundings of reasonably good service would be a boon, often
do not want, or their parents do not want, either to put off their
time of earning or to pay for their training. Day training is not
enough for many of these, and residential training is expensive,
whoever pays for it. Further there is only scanty provision of
such training for well-behaved girls, as distinct from those who are
sent to Homes because they are unmanageable.

(c) Girls trained for six months after leaving school are very
often not fit, physically or morally, to take a good place in service
at fourteen and a half. If they wait about, they forget their

training even as they forget so much of their day school teaching. But public opinion does not yet seem ready to keep them at school till fifteen. These difficulties are not insuperable, but they need consideration. Both the philanthropic training homes, with their accumulated practical experience, and the educational enthusiasts with their hopeful theories have much to learn from each other.

APPENDIX II

SERVICE v. OTHER WORK.

All the servants circularised were asked—"Did you ever work otherwise than in domestic service?" Below are summarised forty replies, which seem to bear out, once more, that the pros and cons of domestic service as compared with "trade" depend chiefly on the worker's personality.

CONTENTED.

FORMER WORK.	PRESENT WORK.
	Housemaid, aged 46, at £22.
1 year in shop.	
Dressmaker.	
5 years in business.	Houseparlourmaid, entered service at 18, now 37.
1½ years dressmaker.	Parlourmaid at £28.
Dressmaker ; 2 years a stewardess.	(Widow at 25.) Nurse at £24 ; prefers this to previous work.
In printing works 1 year.	
In the fields before leaving school.	
6 months in shop.	Parlourmaid (service too dull).
Worked temporarily in laundry.	Hampstead general at £20.
Dressmaking.	Parlourmaid.
Office work for 5 years.	Kitchenmaid. Entered service at 18. Wages £26. Would advise others to enter service for sake of good discipline and chance of saving.
Pupil teacher, 2 years.	In service.
Collar machinist.	Cook at £28.
Worked in the fields till 18.	London general of 38 at £18. 6-10 p.m. out on Sunday, 4-10 p.m. once a week, a fortnight's holiday plus one day a month free.
8 years in paper mill (sorter).	General to 1 lady. Aged 35. Wages £20. Entered service at 11, and has spent 16 years in it.

Former Work.	Present Work.
4 years dressmaking.	Entered service at 20. Now cook-housekeeper of 38 at £50.
3 years dressmaking.	Entered service at 19. Nurse of 25 at £24.
Worked in fields.	Cook-general at £18. Started service at 13½ years.
Worked in silk mill from 13–22.	General, aged 31, or companion help, near Manchester.
Laundry till 18.	Now a general of 23, at £14 10s.
Waistcoat-maker to 19½.	Houseparlourmaid at £20 a year (but complains of loss of caste).

DOUBTFUL.

Dressmaker a few weeks. 6 months in Servants' Employment Agency.	Widow of 34. Supply Cook.
In a tea-room.	Daily at 6s. and food.
In dairy shop and now again in shop after 8 years (from 15–23), in service.	Would very doubtfully recommend.

DISCONTENTED.

Pupil teacher.	Cook, aged 24, at £26.
Dressmaker a few weeks.	
2 years in factories.	Daily general maid.
3 years wigmaking.	Parlourmaid of 25, with 6 other servants. Earns £24.
	Housemaid, 12s. 6d. a week.
Worked at printer's and in tea-rooms before 16, but wages not enough.	
School teaching until 17.	Cook, aged 45, at £24.
Dressmaking.	Housemaid, 35, at £26.
Goldblocking to 16.	Housemaid of 24, at £20. Hard work and confinement the drawbacks.
Dressmaking to 17.	Cook at £25, after 23 years. "Trade or office better, if home good."
	Entered service at 17.
Dressmaking, 2 years.	Cook at £36. Entered service at 20.
(1) Pupil teacher 3 years. (2) in business.	
Peapicking, etc. "Only when I went into the fields to pick peas to earn enough money for my outfit, father being too poor to do it for me."	Nurse at £35. Aged 30, lived in country, 7 miles from town.

APPENDIX III

BY-LAWS AS TO EMPLOYMENT AGENCIES

LONDON COUNTY COUNCIL (GENERAL POWERS) ACT, 1910.

BY-LAWS made by the LONDON COUNTY COUNCIL at a meeting held at the County Hall, Spring Gardens, on Tuesday and Wednesday, the 2nd and 3rd days of April, 1912, with respect to EMPLOYMENT AGENCIES in the ADMINISTRATIVE COUNTY OF LONDON (exclusive of the City of London).

For regulating the conduct of employment agencies.

1. Throughout these by-laws the following words and expressions shall, unless the context otherwise requires, have the meanings hereafter assigned to them, that is to say—

The " Council " means the " London County Council."

" Agent " means a person licensed by the Council to carry on an employment agency.

" Applicant " means and includes both an applicant seeking an employer and an applicant seeking an employee.

" Register " means and includes a book, card or form.

" Preliminary fees " means and includes any fee, audition fee, commission, deposit or monetary payment required or accepted from an applicant either in connection with the registration of the application or for any service connected with such application before the applicant has accepted employment or entered into the situation procured or has been otherwise suited.

" The premises " means and includes the premises specified in the licence of the agent and any other premises used for the purposes of or in connection with his business.

2. No agent shall demand or receive from any applicant payment of any fee or charge unless he shall previously have furnished to such applicant printed or written particulars of his fees or charges, or, if the fee or charge is paid at the premises by the applicant in person, unless his scale of fees or charges is exhibited in such a position that it can be read by the applicant in that part of the premises in which payment is made.

3. An agent shall within seven days of the receipt of a licence to carry on an agency furnish the Council with a copy of his scale of fees or charges and shall not substitute therefor any other fees or charges without first giving notice in writing of the same to the Council.

4. No agent shall receive any preliminary fee from any applicant

who applies to an agent in respect of and in response to an advertisement of a vacant situation.

5. No agent shall in any advertisement, circular, contract or other document issued or made by him or on his behalf or by any verbal representation made by him or on his behalf in connection with his business knowingly deceive or attempt to deceive or cause to be deceived any applicant.

6. An agent shall in every advertisement or circular issued in connection with his business notify that he is an agent, and shall keep on the premises a copy of every such advertisement or circular for a period of twelve months from the date of the issue of such advertisement or circular.

7. No agent shall arrange for the employment abroad of any female person unless he is in possession of information obtained from a responsible person or society or from some other trustworthy source testifying to the satisfactory nature of the proposed employment.

8. No agent shall propose or arrange for the employment abroad of a female person under the age of sixteen years without first obtaining the sanction in writing of her parents or lawful guardian, and unless he has satisfied himself that suitable arrangements have been made for the welfare of such person during the continuance of such employment, and for her return to this country on the conclusion of such employment, and that such employment is legal in the country in which the employment is to take place ; and on making an engagement with such person he shall furnish to her free of cost a written document containing the provisions of this by-law, and stating that such provisions have been complied with. The agent shall in any particular case if so required by the Council furnish the Council with full particulars of the arrangements.

9. An agent shall in every case in which he arranges for the employment abroad of any person, or for the employment in this country of any person resident abroad, furnish such person free of charge with a copy of the contract or other document showing the terms and conditions of such employment drawn up in a language understood by such person.

10. No agent shall make or cause to be made any false entry in any register, receipt, commission note or other document required to be kept, furnished, exhibited, drawn up, prepared or executed in pursuance of these by-laws.

11. If an agent provides upon the premises sleeping accommodation or lodging for any female applicant, he

(a) Shall not suffer any room used by such female applicant for sleeping to be so occupied that there will be in such room less than 350 cubic feet of air space for each person accommodated therein.

(b) Shall keep exhibited in such room a legible notice stating the total number of persons which such room will accommodate in conformity with this by-law.

(c) Shall keep such room furnished with separate bedsteads and sufficient suitable bedding for the number of persons which such room will accommodate in conformity with this by-law.

(d) Shall not cause or suffer any bed in such room to be occupied at any one time by more than one person.

(e) Shall not suffer any male person, other than a person in charge of the premises, to be in that part of any premises which female applicants are for the time being using for sleeping accommodation.

12. An agent (other than an agent in connection with whose business no preliminary fees are demanded or received and who makes each transaction with an applicant the subject of a contract in writing) shall keep a register of applications made by employers, and shall enter therein particulars of every application as to employment he receives, and shall include in such particulars (a) a reference number against the name of each applicant, (b) the date of registration, (c) the name and address of the applicant, (d) the nature of the employment, (e) the salary, wages or terms offered, (f) the amount of any fee paid or payment made by the applicant, and the number of the receipt given for such fee or payment, (g) the name of every person seeking employment, who is either named to the applicant or to whom particulars of the employment are given, and (h) if an engagement has been made the name of the person engaged and the reference number against the name of that person in the register of applications made by persons seeking employment. Such agent shall either keep the applications he receives in alphabetical order, or keep a correct alphabetical index of such applications.

13. An agent (other than an agent in connection with whose business no preliminary fees are demanded or received, and who makes each transaction with an applicant the subject of a contract in writing) shall keep a register of applications made by persons seeking employment and shall enter therein particulars of every application for employment he receives, and shall include in such particulars (a) a reference number against the name of each applicant, (b) the date of registration, (c) the name, address and age of the applicant, (d) the nature of the employment desired, (e) the salary, wages or terms desired, (f) the amount of any fee paid or payment made by the applicant and the number of the receipt given for such fee or payment, (g) the names and addresses of previous employers and the nature or character of the last employment, (h) the name of every employer who is named to the applicant or to whom the name of the applicant is given, and (i) the name and address of the employer engaging and the reference number against the name of such employer in the register of applications made by employers. Such agent shall either keep the applications he receives in alphabetical order, or keep a correct alphabetical index of such applications.

14. An agent (other than an agent in connection with whose business no preliminary fees are demanded or received, and who makes each transaction with an applicant the subject of a con-

tract in writing) shall keep a book of forms of numbered receipts and counterfoils and shall issue a receipt in respect of every payment or deposit made by an applicant, and shall enter on such receipt and the counterfoil thereof his trade name and address, the date of payment and the reference number of the applicant in the register of applications made by employers or the register of applications made by persons seeking employment, and, where the payment is an engagement fee, the nature of the employment offered to the applicant and the wages and emoluments attaching thereto.

15. An agent in connection with whose business no preliminary fees are demanded or received, and who makes each transaction with an applicant the subject of a contract in writing, shall in every such transaction correctly indicate in the contract or commission note the following particulars—

(a) The name and address of the applicant.
(b) The name of the person with whom the engagement of the applicant is made.
(c) The place at which the engagement is to be fulfilled.
(d) The salary to be paid to the applicant.
(e) The commission to be paid to the agent.
(f) The conditions under which any future commission to the agent will be payable.

The agent shall provide a copy of such contract or commission note to the applicant and shall keep a copy on the premises for a period of not less than twelve months, and he shall also keep all such contracts or commission notes or copies thereof correctly indexed and in order of date or arranged alphabetically according to the name of the applicant.

16. A theatrical, variety or concert agent shall keep a complete list of children under the age of 16 years who are booked by him for engagements either in London or elsewhere, and shall in such list indicate the place or places of entertainment at which each child is booked to perform and the length of engagement of each child at each such place of entertainment.

17. From and after the date of the confirmation of these by-laws, the by-laws relating to employment agencies, which were made by the Council on the 18th day of December, 1906, pursuant to section 47 of the London County Council (General Powers) Act, 1905, shall be revoked.

Sealed by order,

L.S.   LAURENCE GOMME,
Clerk of the Council.

I hereby confirm the foregoing By-Laws.
Dated 10th August, 1912.

R. McKENNA,
L.S.   *One of His Majesty's*
Principal Secretaries of State.

APPENDIX IV

SPECIMEN REGULATIONS AS TO UNDERGROUND
BEDROOMS

Regulations prescribed by the Mayor, Aldermen and Councillors of
the Royal Borough of Kensington, under Section 17 (7) of the
Housing, Town Planning, etc., Act, 1909.

A room habitually used as a sleeping place, the surface of the
floor of which is more than three feet below the surface of the part
of the street adjoining or nearest to the room, shall comply with
the following regulations, namely :—

(a) Every wall of such room shall be constructed with a proper
damp-proof course, and, if in contact with the soil, shall be
effectually protected against dampness from that soil by means
of a vertical damp-proof course or otherwise.

(b) An area or open space shall adjoin the room and extend
either throughout the entire length of one side thereof, or at least
throughout the entire width of any window or windows required
by these regulations and (except where the area of such window
or windows shall be of not less extent than one-seventh of the
floor area of the room) for distances on both sides of such window
or windows which together amount to a distance of five feet.

Such area or open space shall not be less than two feet wide in
every part thereof and shall be open upwards from a level three
inches below the level of the damp-proof course in the adjoining wall
of the room.

In the case of an area, the same shall be properly paved with
impervious material and effectually drained by means of a properly
trapped gully.

Provided (a) that where a bay window having side lights adjoins
such area the width thereof in front of the central light may be one
foot at the least, and (b) that any steps necessary for access to any
part of the building comprising the room may be placed in or over
such area if they are so placed as not to be over or across any window
of the room required by the regulation in that behalf.

Provided further that this regulation shall not apply to a room
which is adequately lighted by means of a top light or top lights
and is provided with adequate means of ventilation.

(c) The sub-soil of the site of such room shall be effectually
drained by means of a sub-soil drain properly trapped and
ventilated wherever the dampness of the site renders such a pre-
caution necessary.

(d) The space (if any) beneath the floor of such room shall be provided with adequate means of ventilation.

(e) Every drain passing under such room, other than a drain for the drainage of the sub-soil of the site of such room, shall be properly constructed of a gas-tight pipe.

(f) Such room shall be effectually protected against the rising of any effluvia or exhalation by means of a layer of asphalte or of good concrete at least six inches thick, or four inches thick if properly grouted, laid upon the soil of the site of the entire room, or in some equally effectual manner.

(g) If such room is without a fireplace and a flue properly constructed and properly connected with such fireplace, it shall be provided with special and adequate means of ventilation by a sufficient aperture or air shaft, which shall provide an unobstructed sectional area of 81 square inches at the least.

(h) (i.) Such room shall be effectually lighted by means of one or more windows opening directly into the external air.

(ii.) Every such window shall be so constructed that one half at the least may be opened, and that the opening may extend to the top of the window.

(iii.) The total area of such window or windows clear of the sash frames shall be equal at least to one-tenth of the floor area of the room.

(iv.) A portion of such total area equal in extent to at least one-twelfth of such floor area shall be so situated that a line making an angle of thirty degrees with a horizontal plane can be drawn upwards from any point thereon in a vertical plane at right angles to the plane of the window so as not to intersect within a distance of ten feet measured horizontally from the window any wall of any area adjoining the room or any other wall or any kerb or other obstruction except an open fence.

(v.) In estimating the area of a window or windows for the purpose of this regulation no account shall be taken of any part of any such window which is above the mean level of the ceiling of the room.

(vi.) Any such window or windows shall overlook the area or open space referred to in these regulations.

Provided that the paragraphs numbered (ii.), (iv.), (v.) and (vi.) of this regulation shall not apply to a room which is adequately lighted by means of a top light or top lights and is provided with adequate means of ventilation and that for the purposes of the paragraphs numbered (iii.) and (iv.) of this regulation a bay window having side lights shall be assumed to be equivalent to a flat window of the same area and of the same height in relation to the room and situated at a distance from the outside area wall equal to the mean width of the area,

The Common Seal of the Mayor, Aldermen and Councillors
of the Royal Borough of Kensington was hereunto affixed   L.S.
the Twenty-fifth day of February One thousand nine
hundred and thirteen in the presence of
(Signed) WM. CHAMBERS LEETE,
Town Clerk.

The Consent of the Local Government Board is hereby
given to the foregoing Regulations this Seventeenth day   L.S.
of April, 1913.
(Signed) H. C. MONRO, *Secretary.*
Acting on behalf of the said Board under
the authority of their General Order
dated the Twenty-sixth
day of May, 1877.

APPENDIX V

LABOUR EXCHANGE STATISTICS AND REGULATIONS WITH
REGARD TO SERVICE

Extract from report on Work of Board of Trade Labour Exchanges
in 1914.

Number of applicants for employment in Domestic Service.
(N.B.—This includes "laundry and washing" service.)

	Women.			Girls.	
	1913.	1914.		1913.	1914.
	178,256	225,662	..		
Vacancies filled ..	102,717	120,514	..	20,181	23,717
No. of individuals placed	77,703	88,664	..	17,334	20,623

Since August, 1914, the Labour Exchanges have been empowered
to supply servants in private houses, but, in the case of juvenile
applicants, under the restrictions given below.

Conditions on which Advisory Committees for Juvenile Employment are allowed to place juvenile applicants in resident Domestic
Service for private houses.

(a) No placing must be done by a Labour Exchange Officer
without the advice of at least one member of the committee or a
co-opted member of a rota or sub-committee.

(b) The committee will undertake to arrange co-operation with
any satisfactory voluntary agencies engaged in this kind of work
in their district; and will undertake, either by themselves or
through such agencies, to enquire into vacancies offered and to
provide for regular after-supervision in all cases when it is desirable.

(c) The committee will agree not to advertise this work at the
expense of other branches of their work.

In London the work of placing girls under seventeen in domestic
service (to live in) is entrusted by the Juvenile Advisory Committees
to the Metropolitan Association for Befriending Young Servants;
in the provinces, girls are placed in domestic service only in those
Labour Exchange districts (at present 85 in number) where the
Juvenile Employment Committee or Juvenile Advisory Committee
has passed a definite resolution to that effect on the lines of the
" conditions " printed above. In some districts a special sub-
committee verifies these situations, in others the committee itself
is responsible ; but in no case may the woman clerk alone send a
girl under seventeen to a situation in private service.

APPENDIX VI

Extracts from Census Returns of 1911. Vol. X. Pt. I.

Introduction pp. xxiv. ff.

IV.—Domestic and Other Allied Services.—The number of persons classified in this order was 2,121,717, of whom 387,677 were males and 1,734,040 females. These numbers include persons engaged in (1) domestic indoor service, whether in private families, in business establishments, or in hotels, lodging houses, etc. ; (2) domestic outdoor service ; and (3) other allied services. This last includes, amongst others, laundry workers and charwomen, and may be disregarded for the purposes of this enquiry.

The totals in 1901 and 1911 for the three sub-orders, including "Day Girls, Day Servants" in the first sub-order were as follows :—

	1901.		
	Persons.	Males.	Females.
1. Domestic indoor service (including day girls)	1,394,929	64,146	1,330,783
2. Domestic outdoor service	179,968	179,932	36
3. Other service	420,020	60,117	359,903
Total	1,994,917	304,195	1,690,722

	1911.		Increase per cent.
	Males.	Females.	
1. Domestic indoor service (including day girls)	54,260	1,359,359	1·3
2. Domestic outdoor service..	226,266	104	25·8
3. Other service	107,151	374,577	14·7
Total	387,677	1,734,040	6·4

The number of Domestic Indoor Servants has increased at a much lower rate since 1901 than has the general population.

The average number of persons per family had declined from 4.62 in 1901 to 4.51 in 1911, and it was, therefore, to be anticipated that on this account the proportion of servants per 1000 families would have tended to decrease. The following figures show that not only is this the case, but that there has also been an appreciable decrease per 1000 population :—

	1881.	1901.	1911.
Families or Separate Occupiers	5,633,192	7,036,868	8,005,290
Population	25,974,439	32,527,843	36,070,492
Female Domestic Indoor Servants	1,230,406	1,330,783	1,359,359
Female Domestic Indoor Servants, per 1,000 Families	218	189	170
Female Domestic Indoor Servants, per 1,000 Population	47	41	38

It was shown in the Report on the Census of 1901 that an examination of the age-distribution of female domestic indoor servants as returned in 1881 and 1901 suggested a disinclination on the part of young women for domestic service, and the continuation of this tendency is clearly demonstrated in the following table, in which "Day Girls, Day Servants," are included, for purposes of comparison, in the figures for 1911.

TABLE VI.—AGES OF FEMALE DOMESTIC INDOOR SERVANTS, 1881, 1901 AND 1911.

Ages.	Female Domestic Indoor Servants.						Increase or Decrease per cent.
	Numbers.			Proportions per 1000.			
	1881.	1901.	1911.	1881.	1901.	1911.	1901–1911
Total... ...	1,230,406	1,330,783	1,359,359	1000·	1000·	1000·	+ 2·1
10 to 14 ⎫	98,190	20,034	7,466 ⎫	79·8	15·1	5·5	—62·7
14 ... ⎭		44,768	37,049 ⎭		33·6	27·3	—17·2
15 to 20 ...	430,177	398,630	390,330	349·7	299·6	287·1	— 2·1
20 to 25 ...	301,474	351,242	345,251	245·0	263·9	254·0	— 3·7
25 to 35 ⎫	295,302	279,881	300,310 ⎫	240·0	210·3	220·9	+ 7·3
35 to 45 ⎭		113,092	134,970 ⎭		85·0	99·3	+19·3
45 to 55 ...	88,506	67,605	83,104 ⎫	71·9	50·8	61·1	+22·9
55 to 65 ...		38,581	43,206 ⎭		29·0	31·8	+12·0
65 and upwards	16,757	16,950	17,673	13·6	12·7	13·0	+ 4·3

The very large reduction in the proportion at the youngest age-group shown in the table is undoubtedly due mainly to the general raising of the age at which children leave school. But the limitation of juvenile employment from this cause does not appear to have affected to any appreciable extent the total number occupied at the age 14—15, and the decline of 17·2 per cent. shown in the table must, therefore, be attributed to a preference at this age for other forms of occupation rather than to a prolongation of school life. At ages 20—25 there has been a fall of 1·7 per cent. in the numbers between 1901 and 1911, and the total decline at all ages up to 25 has amounted to 34,578 or 4·2 per cent. ; while above 25 years there has been an increase at each age-period in the table, reaching a maximum of 22·9 per cent. at 45—55, and amounting altogether to 63,154 or 12·2 per cent.

The increase in the number of female domestic indoor servants between 1901 and 1911 in the aggregate of all the rural districts was at the rate of 5·5 per cent. . . . Taking the number of servants in proportion to population it is found that, while in the urban districts it showed a distinct fall from 39 to 36 per 1,000, it was practically stationary at 45 per 1,000 in the rural districts.

TABLE VIII.—FEMALE DOMESTIC INDOOR SERVANTS PER 1,000 FAMILIES IN CERTAIN COUNTIES, 1911.

Low Proportions of Servants in 1911.		High Proportions of Servants in 1911.	
Administrative County.	Per 1,000 Families.	Administrative County.	Per 1,000 Families.
Lancashire	97	Montgomeryshire	214
Yorks, West Riding	100	Dorsetshire	216
Durham	102	Oxfordshire	218
Glamorganshire	112	Westmorland	219
Monmouthshre	115	Kent	224
Derbyshire	119	Shropshire	224
Nottinghamshire	127	Wight, Isle of	231
Leicestershire	131	Radnorshire	234
Staffordshire	135	Southampton	237
Northamptonshire	142	Yorks, East Riding	240
Ely, Isle of	146	Hertfordshire	241
Peterborough, Soke of	148	Herefordshire	246
Carmarthenshire	148	Devonshire	247
Lincolnshire (Holland)	149	Rutlandshire	255
Northumberland	151	Sussex, West	277
Essex	154	Berkshire	278
Cumberland	155	Sussex, East	331
Cornwall	157	Surrey	353

Among the County Boroughs and other towns of over 50,000 population the proportions varied more widely than in the Administrative Counties ; there were less than 100 servants per 1,000 families in 41 of these towns, the lowest proportions being 38 in Aston Manor, 45 in Burnley, 49 in Rochdale, 51 in Blackburn and in Oldham, 57 in Preston, 59 in Smethwick and in Dewsbury, and 60 in Bolton and in Bury, while in 9 of the largest towns the proportions were not less than 300 per 1,000, viz., 300 in Oxford, 304 in Hastings, 305 in Southport, 307 in Bath, 335 in Hornsey, 358 in Wimbledon, 403 in Ealing, 408 in Eastbourne, and 415 in Bournemouth. Among the Metropolitan Boroughs the extremes ranged from 35 in Bethnal Green, 39 in Shoreditch, 42 in Bermondsey, 50 in Finsbury, 51 in Southwark, 54 in Poplar, and 64 in Stepney, to 408 in Paddington, 483 in St. Marylebone, 544 in Chelsea, 545 in the City of Westminster, 707 in Kensington and 737 in Hampstead.

APPEN

SUMMARY OF REPLIES TO ENQUIRIES FROM

Place.	Is there difficulty in obtaining servants for hotel work?	If so, reason.
1. Glasgow	Yes. Equal difficulty in finding hotel servants and private servants.	Increased openings for female labour, and probably particularly to emigration, appealing to the love of change and the romantic.
2. Inverness	No.	
3. Farnborough	Very little.	
4. Aberdeen	Only during summer months	Supply not equal to demand.
5. Letchworth	In the case of scullery and kitchenmaids, and in other respects.	In view of the openings as housemaids, the kitchen duties are hard and the hours long; they prefer the former calling and factory work.
6. Liverpool	No.	
7. Brighton	No.	

DIX VII

HOTEL-KEEPERS IN DIFFERENT PARTS.

If not, reason for greater popularity of hotel service over private service.

Regular hours on and off duty. Having specific work. Tips. One master, company of fellow servants.

1. Pay with the addition of tips. 2. A larger number of servants together. 3. Male staff. 4. And here the soldier servants of officers. 5. Absence of interference in work. 6. Fixed time off duty.

The greater " expectations " of life among domestics and the excitement of hotel life as compared with private service. Tips, regular time " off " daily. Greater variety.

Better hours, gratuities and discipline.

Fixed time being allowed for their leisure each day, and " tips " which add considerably to wages.

8. Bridge of Allan	Good ones, Yes. Bad ones, No.	Both domestic and hotel servants ought to have Employment Books somewhat similar to the Seamen's Board of Trade continuous discharge books and they ought to have some schools where they can be properly trained. I commend to your notice the system of Government Employment books in use in Switzerland.
9. Folkestone ..	Not house and chambermaids.	
10. Tunbridge Wells	No.	
11. Newmarket ..	Men, Yes (present time). Women, No.	Men enlisting.
12. Sheffield ..	No.	
13. Wells	No.	
14. London, S.W. ..	Yes, good ones.	They like to to be free in the evening.
15. Nottingham ..	No great difficulty.	
16. London, S.W. ..	None whatsoever.	
17. Bexhill	No.	

There is more change and the employment is less of a drudgery and more interesting, and usually is better paid after tips are taken into account.

Can make more money and get more time off duty.

Women being thrown out of employment owing to reduction of expenses in households.

Tips. Variety and excitement of hotel life. The companionship of numerous other servants. More liberty and outings.

More money made.

Higher wages as a rule. More brightness in the life and always a change of visitors and a good deal of money in tips, or perquisites. More varied food.

---

1. Servants are kept to a proper time sheet, and know exactly when they are off duty, which often varies in private houses. 2. They have an opportunity of earning more money. 3. They have more company, which in the case of female servants may be of matrimonial interest.

The life generally is brighter and easier hours of service. The hotel servant has from two to three hours off duty a day, and one long evening per week and in some cases Sunday evening.

18. Canterbury	..	Yes, competent ones.	They earn too much to-day and get situations without references or characters. This is affected by hop-picking, also by presence of military.
19. Basingstoke	..	I had. A servant who will do her work, however passably, is never discharged.	It is incurable thriftlessness and instability of character. Tips are prevalent here, but as long as servants can get sufficient to dress upon and to visit the cinema they are satisfied. They see nothing beyond the week. They take their situations when they are hungry, and become independent when they have appeased their appetites. It is not a matter of wages. I insist on a long notice, and as it is impossible for them to look a month ahead I have no trouble now.
20. Droitwich	..	*Not generally.* Supply very limited for the undermaids, for house cleaning and looking after staff rooms, etc.	
21. Haslemere	..	Yes, in finding competent ones.	They do not like coming to the country, especially in winter.
22. Kensington	..	No : occasionally there is a scarcity, generally in the Spring when all the season hotels open.	

It is certainly much easier to get servants for hotels than for private families—they do not work so hard, they have more liberty and it is a more cheerful existence than being shut up in a kitchen all day.

The usual short notice prevalent in hotels enables servants to satisfy their craving for frequent change. A good servant has the disease, but gets over it, and usually applies to resume her situation on a vacancy occurring, a bad one never.

The wages as a rule are comparatively better and the majority receive also recognition from visitors—the food is usually more liberal and varied, and the company of so many other servants and more frequent and regular off duty times are two considerations which they appreciate. The duties are usually more definitely arranged, and meal hours regular of household and themselves.

Those who do settle down have the advantage of definite duties, regular times off duty and the opportunity of adding greatly to their wages by presents in money from visitors.

More outings and off-duty ; more regular duties ; better remuneration (taking into consideration gratuities); the life is more attractive.

23. Plymouth   .. No.

24. Manchester, London, Liverpool, Leeds, Bradford, Derby, etc.	It is always diffi- cult to get first class servants, but there is no difficulty in fil- ling the places of those of the ordinary staff who leave from time to time.	
25. Llandudno .. No.		
26. Weybridge .. Yes.		Does not know.

I should think that after an hotel, private houses for servants must be dull, lack of company, excessive hours, not set work, whereas in hotels they all have their set work, sociability, better hours, more off-duty and in many cases more money.

More regular hours off duty, and consequently a greater amount of freedom and the means of augmenting their wages by gratuities from visitors.

Greater freedom. Higher wages.

APPENDIX VIII

DOMESTIC SERVICE ENQUIRY.

The Form sent to Servants.

July, 1913.

DEAR MADAM,

We are making an enquiry into the conditions of Domestic Service. Every occupation in life has its drawbacks, and we want you to tell us straight out what you would like altered, and if possible, how you think the alterations could be made, because you know both the good and the bad side of service.

If you are not able to reply to all the questions, just answer those that interest you, and let us have your replies as soon as possible. Please number your answers to match the questions.

We should like to have your name and address, but we shall not make them known unless you give us special permission to do so, and anything you tell us is quite confidential.

If you have any friends who will answer the questions, will you please send their names and addresses to Miss Butler, Women's Industrial Council, 7, John Street, Strand, W.C., so that she may send them these questions.

We ask your help because we mean to try and make things better, and the first thing to do is to find out exactly where the shoe pinches; this can only be told us by those who have themselves been in service.

We are,

Yours faithfully,

CLEMENTINA BLACK, Chairman.
MAY S. BARLOW, Hon. Sec., Domestic Service Sub-Committee.
L. WYATT PAPWORTH, Secretary and Treasurer.

NAMES AND ADDRESSES WILL NOT BE MADE KNOWN WITHOUT SPECIAL PERMISSION

1. Name.
2. Address.
3. What is your branch of service (as cook, parlourmaid, general servant, daily servant, etc.) ? Please say which.

4. How many servants are there in your employer's house ?
Men.
Women.
5. Were your father or your mother in service before you ?
6. Did you have any training before you went to your first place ?
7. What age were you when you went to your first place ?
8. Who provided the outfit ?
9. How long have you been in service ?
10. What are your wages ?
11. How much free time have you each day
   (1) out of the house ?
   (2) in the house ?
12. How much free time have you on Sundays ?
   (1) out of the house ?
   (2) in the house ?
13. Have you a bed to yourself ?
14. How long holidays have you in the year ?
15. Are your wages paid during your holidays ?
16. Why did you go into service ?
17. Have you ever worked anywhere except in service ?
18. Would you advise any young friend to go into service ? If not, why not ?
19. What do you think could be done to make domestic service a more desirable occupation ?
20. Did you belong to a girls' club when you left school ?
21. Name of any club, society, or association which you may have joined since you have been in service ?
22. Can you spend your free time at such a club ?
23. Do you belong to a union or friendly society, or sick club ?
24. What do you think about registry offices ?

THE FORM SENT TO MISTRESSES.

DEAR MADAM,

We are making an Enquiry into the Conditions of Domestic Service—the largest single industry in this country. We have drawn up, from various sources, a list both of the alleged drawbacks to domestic service and of reforms which have been suggested. These we have grouped under four heads :—

   (a) Complete absence of organization in the Trade.
   (b) Wages.
   (c) Disadvantages of Domestic Service as compared with other Trades.
   (d) Prospects.

We invite you most heartily to co-operate with us by commenting on these suggestions, and by making any others which may occur to you as solutions of the difficulty, so that the resulting information may be used as a basis for action which will benefit both employer and employed.

Kindly write your name and address below. No names will be published without special permission. It will much simplify the work of tabulation if you will kindly make your comments on this form.

We are,
      Yours faithfully,

CLEMENTINA BLACK, Chairman of Investigation Committee.
MAY S. BARLOW, Hon. Sec., Domestic Service Sub-Committee.
L. WYATT PAPWORTH, Secretary and Treasurer.

NOTE—The Council has incorporated all suggestions received to date, and is not responsible for any of them. [1]

A. COMPLETE ABSENCE OF ORGANIZATION IN THE TRADE.

1. REGISTRY OFFICES.—Generally speaking the registry office system as at present conducted is not satisfactory. The persons in charge of the offices make their living out of fees paid by employer and employed and, in consequence, the greater number of changes of situation the girls make the larger is the income of the registry office proprietor.

Suggestions.—(*a*) A strict system of licensing and supervision of registry offices is recommended ; (*b*) The work should be transferred to Labour Exchange authorities.

2. INEFFICIENCY.—Inefficiency on the part of the Employer. The training of mistresses in domestic subjects has often been neglected.

Suggestion.—(*a*) There should be increased facilities for domestic training.

Inefficiency on the part of the Servant. There is no standard of training or efficiency or requirements.

Suggestions.—(*b*) Domestic training should be included as a compulsory subject in the elementary Schools ; (*c*) Trade Schools and continuation classes should be established after the elementary school age for the special purpose of training for domestic service.

3. INDEFINITE TERMS OF ENGAGEMENT.—The contract is indefinite as regards the work required of the servant and as to the accommodation, food and holiday provided.

Suggestion.—The contract should be more definite on both sides and should include a regular annual holiday, with wages, after a certain length of service.

4. REFERENCES.—A mistress cannot always obtain a reference with a new servant.

A servant cannot claim a character when leaving a situation.

A servant has no recognized means of obtaining information as to the household she is going to enter.

---

[1] Space was left on the Schedules sent to mistresses for written comments on each group of statements and suggestions here printed.

Suggestions.—(*a*) Some official organization should hold all references on both sides; (*b*) The Labour Exchanges should hold all references.

5. ABSENCE OF TRADE ORGANIZATION.—The trade is practically unorganized.

Suggestions.—(*a*) Organizations could be formed, one for mistresses and one for servants; (*b*) An organization could be formed to which mistresses and servants could belong.

B. WAGES, &c.

1. NO STANDARD OF WAGES.—There is no standard of wages asked or offered in relation to a standard of efficiency.

Suggestions.—(*a*) A minimum wage for all servants should be established by law; (*b*) An organization of servants should be formed guaranteeing the efficiency of its members, and in return receiving a wage above the minimum.

2. HIRE PURCHASE SYSTEM.—Lowers the moral fibre.

Suggestion.—It should be illegal to sell goods on the hire purchase system to servants.

3. SECRET COMMISSIONS.—Lower the moral fibre.

Suggestion.—The provisions of the Prevention of Corruption Act, 1906, should be enforced.

C. DISADVANTAGES OF DOMESTIC SERVICE AS COMPARED WITH OTHER TRADES.

1. LESS LIBERTY.—The girls employed in factories, shops, etc., are able to spend their evenings and nights at home. They are at home on Sundays and they have a half-holiday during the week. Servants who "live in" have, on an average, half of Sunday and one evening a week to themselves. Daily servants live at home, but it is said that the conditions of their homes are often such that employers do not care to employ servants coming from them.

Suggestions.—(*a*) More girls should be trained for *daily* service, and employers should be induced to engage this class of worker; (*b*) The home conditions should be improved by the work of such organizations as the School Care Committee; (*c*) Servants "living in" should have a definite allowance of free time every day; (*d*) Hostels of residence might be established where these daily servants could live.

2. LESS COMPANIONSHIP.—Girls working in factories and shops have the companionship of their fellow workers during the day. It is only in large establishments that servants can get companionship of their equals to any considerable extent. They cannot choose their fellow workers.

Suggestions.—(*a*) There should be a greater number of social clubs for servants where they can go on their free evenings and on Sundays, and where they can meet their friends; (*b*) Some arrangement should be devised by which servants might safely receive visits from their friends and relatives.

3. LESS WAGES BROUGHT HOME AT FIRST.—At present girls usually leave school when they are 14 or under. This age is too low to admit a girl to *good* service—but, at this age, a girl can earn 4/- to 5/- a week at a factory or shop. This induces parents to send their daughters to a factory or shop instead of to a situation where the earnings are small.

Suggestion.—The school-leaving age should be increased by two years during which a trade should be learnt. A girl of sixteen could get into a good situation if thus trained for domestic service, and could earn as much, if not more, than she could in any other trade. Only in very exceptional cases is domestic service a suitable occupation for girls under sixteen years.

4. DIFFICULTY IN PROVIDING OUTFIT.—It is difficult to provide the necessary outfit for the first situation.

Suggestions.—(*a*) This could be met by deposits by the children in school banks ; (*b*) The uniform could be provided by an Apprenticeship Society ; (*c*) Insurance to provide a sum with which an outfit could be bought; (*d*) Outfit could be made in the school sewing class.

5. UNIFORM.—Servants dislike wearing a uniform.

Suggestion.—If a Trade Association were formed of which trained servants were members, the uniform would become a badge of honour and would help to raise the status of the trade, as in the case of hospital nurses.

6. ACCOMMODATION PROVIDED.—Unsatisfactory sleeping accommodation is sometimes provided. The kitchens are often depressing and sometimes insanitary.

Suggestions.—(*a*) There should be a system of inspection of accommodation ; (*b*) Every servant should have a right to a bed to herself ; (*c*) The sleeping and living accommodation should be shown to the servant before the engagement is made.

7. MORAL DANGERS.—Mothers often keep their girls from entering domestic service because they fear they will be less secure than when living at home.

Suggestions.—(*a*) Hygiene and temperance should be taught in the schools ; (*b*) Definite instruction with regard to sex should be given before entering service ; (*c*) If the standard of domestic service were raised the moral tone would also be improved ; (*d*) Feeble-minded persons should be excluded from domestic service.

D. PROSPECTS.

1. A SERVANT HAS NO TRADE AFTER MARRIAGE.—Domestic Service does not so generally provide a woman with a trade by working at which in her home she can augment her husband's wages. The woman who has worked in a factory before marriage can often get work of the same sort to do at home.

Suggestion.—A larger demand for daily servants might enable a greater number of married women and widows to find employment in daily service.

2. A SERVANT HAS LESS OPPORTUNITY FOR MARRIAGE.—The servant has not the same opportunity of meeting men of her own class as the girl working in the factory, the shop, etc. There is also the question of status. There is a belief that a man looks down on a girl who is in service but not on her sister in the shop. The servant is regarded as a person of lower social rank than many other workers (*e.g.*, shop assistants, clerks), as shown by the use of the Christian name.

Suggestions.—(a) By bringing Domestic Service more into line with other trades, and by educating the public into considering that it is a highly honourable career for women, much could be done towards making it more popular ; (b) Servants should be called by official titles. What do you suggest ?

3. A SERVANT IS LESS WELL-ADAPTED FOR A WORKING-CLASS HOME AFTER MARRIAGE.—A highly specialised servant is not adapted to the requirements of a working-class home after marriage. Servants have been in the habit of living at other people's expense and are not used to administering money.

Suggestion.—If servants were employed to do some of the household buying they would gain experience.

4. ABSENCE OF ANY PROVISION FOR THE FUTURE.—An old servant who has worked for a family for some years is usually helped by them but there is no definite arrangement. Personal saving is often impossible for servants, because they are almost always helping relations.

Suggestions.—(a) A system of National Insurance ; (b) A bonus should be given for long service.

APPENDIX IX

Bibliography

SERVANTS

ALL THE YEAR ROUND MAGAZINE. *Servants Old and New.* Vol. XVIII., 79.

BOARD OF TRADE. C. 9346. *Report by Miss C. Collet to the Labour Department on the Money Wages of Domestic Servants.* 1899.

T. H. BAYLIS. *Rights, Duties and Relations of Domestic Servants and their Masters and Mistresses.* 69 pp. Sampson Low. 1906.

CARITAS. C. E. HUCH. *Dienstbotennot und Dienstbotenelend.* XV. 10/11. 12.

J. D. CASWELL. *Law of Domestic Servants.* With a Chapter on the National Insurance Act, 1911. Jordan. 1/6. 1913.

L'ACTION POPULAIRE. R. E. CHALAMET. *Les Ouvrières Domestiques.* 34 pp. Paris et Reims. Fr. o.25. n.d.

E. CONRAD. *Das Dienstproblem in den nordamerikanischen Staaten und was es uns lehrt.* III. 43 pp. G. Fischer, Jena. M. 1.20. 1908.

DEFOE. *Great Law of Subordination.* B.M. 522d7.

DEFOE. *Everybody's Business, Nobody's Business (Behaviour of Servants).* B.M. 12331 e 22 (1).

DIE GLEICHHEIT, STUTTGART. TH. SCHLESINGER, *Zur Literatur über die Dienstbotenfrage.* V. 24. 1909.

ERNST. *Die Dienstbotenfrage.* (Bericht über den katholischen Frauentag in Wien.) 1910.

FRANKFURTER ZEITUNG. *Ueberangebot von Dienstboten.* LII. 3 Morgenbl, 6/11, Abendblatt, 7/11. Frankfurt. 1908.

ELSE KERSTEN-CONRAD. *Zur Dienstbotenfrage. Erhebungen der Arbeiterschutz Kommission des Bundes Deutscher Frauenvereine.* Archiv fur Sozialwissenschaft und Sozial Politik. XXXL2. Tübingen. 1910.

KUHLER. *Die Grundlagen der Dienstbotenfrage.* 61 pp. Berlin. 1910.

E. M. MASSEY. *The Rights and Obligations of Domestic Servants.* 46 pages. Mrs. Massey's Agency for Domestic Service, 10, Baker Street, W. 9d. 1914.

DOMESTIC SERVICE. MRS. MASSEY. (A pamphlet.) 10, Baker Street, W. 1d. 1914.

J. MACDONELL. *The Law of Master and Servant.* Butterworth, London. 25/-. 1909.

APPENDIX 147

L'ACTION POPULAIRE. ABBÉ PICQ. *Une Œuvre de Domestiques ruraux.* 32 pp. No. 191. Reims. 1909.

DR. A. PIEPE. *Dientsboten und Dientsbotenvereine.* (Soziale Tagesfragen, No. 21.) M. Gladbach. Volksvereinsverlag. 1908.

DR. LISA ROSS. *Weibliche Dienstboten und Dienstbotenhaltung in England.* Mohr, Tübingen. 1912.

LUCY M. SALMON. *Domestic Service.* Putnams. 1901.

ATLANTIC MONTHLY. LUCY M. SALMON. *Recent Progress in the Study of Domestic Service.* Nov., 1905.

BRITISH ASSOCIATION. LADY KNIGHTLEY OF FAWSLEY. *The Terms and Conditions of Domestic Service in England and in South Africa.* Brief Summary. 1905.

CHAMBERS JOURNAL. KATH. BIRRILL. *The Servant Question Again.* Oct., 1906.

CHARITY ORGANIZATION REVIEW. ALICE MODEL. *The Sick Room Helps Society and the Work.* April, 1914.

CONTEMPORARY REVIEW. LADY BUNTING. *Mistress and Maid.* May, 1910.

ECONOMIC JOURNAL. H. JASTROW. *Domestic Servants in Germany, their economic, legal and social position.* Pp. 625-33. 1899.

ENGLISHWOMAN. H. B. WALLIS CHAPMAN. *The Unorganised Trade.* (Deals with Domestic Service.) Feb., 1913.

GOOD HOUSEKEEPING. P. V. MIGHELS. *The Domestic Servant Problem.* Sept., 1906.

JOURNAL OF POLITICAL ECONOMY. I. M. RUBINOW. *The Problem of Domestic Service.* Pp. 502-19. (American only.) Oct., 1906.

JOURNAL OF ROYAL STATISTICAL SOCIETY. W. T. LAYTON. *Changes in the Wages of Domestic Servants during Fifty Years.* (A note with many tables.) Sept., 1908.

LABOUR LEADER. PRISCILLA MOULDER. *A Union of Domestic Servants.* XXI., 20. 1910.

MUSÉE SOCIALE. MME. MOLL WEISS. *Schools for Servants in Switzerland.* Dec., 1911.

MUSÉE SOCIALE. MME. MOLL WEISS. *Les Ecoles des Servantes en Belgique et en Hollande.* Oct., 1913.

NATIONAL REVIEW. M. E. TYTLER. *The Eternal Servant Problem.* Aug., 1909.

NATIONAL REVIEW. LADY WILLOUGHBY DE BROKE. *Pros and Cons of Domestic Service.* Nov., 1912.

NATIONAL REVIEW. MRS. HOME MCCALL. *Another Aspect of the Servant Problem.* Feb., 1913.

NATIONAL REVIEW. NELLIE ANDERSON. *A Servant's View of the Servants' Problem.* March, 1913.

SOZIALE KULTUR. KULEMANN. *Zur Geschichte der Dienstboten Organisationen.* XXVIII. München, Gladbach. 1908.

SOZIALE PRAXIS, BERLIN. E. GNAUCK-KUHNE. *Dienstbotenmangel und Frauenfrage.* Feb.-March, 1901.

SOZIALE PRAXIS, BERLIN. DR. LEO. *Zur Dienstbotenfrage.* Aug., 1908.

SOZIALE PRAXIS, BERLIN. S. SUSMANN UND G. ZUCHER. *Noch einmal die Dienstbotenfrage.* Aug., 1908.

SOZIALE PRAXIS. DR. W. KAHLER. *Dienstbotenfrage u. Gesindeordnung.* Sept., 1909.

SOZIALE REVUE. A. STUMPF. *Die Dienstbotenfrage. Die Soziale Lage der weiblichendienstboten.* R. BRUCKMAYER. *Welches ist die geeignete Form der Organisation der Dienstmädchen?* Essen. 29 pp. M.o. 50. 1908.

SWIFT. *Directions to Servants.* B.M. 1077. i. 45.

WOMAN AT HOME. MRS. ARNOLD BENNETT. *Solving the Servant Question.* May, 1914.

SOZIALISTISCHE MONATSHEFTE. E. FISCHER. *The Servant Question.* Dec., 1907.

WOMEN'S EMPLOYMENT. *Housecraft as a Profession for Women.* May, 1909.

WOMEN'S INDUSTRIAL NEWS. P. V. MIGHELS. *Domestic Service.* June, 1909.

WOMEN'S INDUSTRIAL NEWS. *Report of a Conference on Training of Children's Nurses.* March, 1904.

WOMEN'S INDUSTRIAL NEWS. *Servants' References.* Sept., 1906.

WOMEN'S INDUSTRIAL NEWS. M. S. BARLOW. *Children's Nurses. Supply and Demand.* July, 1911.

The List of Titles
in the Garland Series

11. Edward G. Howarth and Mona Wilson. **West Ham. A Study in Social and Industrial Problems.** London, 1907.

12. B.L. Hutchins. **Women in Modern Industry.** London, 1915.

13. M. Loane. **From Their Point of View.** London, 1908.

14. J. Ramsay Macdonald. **Women in the Printing Trades. A Sociological Study.** London, 1904.

15. C.F.G. Masterman. **From the Abyss. Of Its Inhabitants by One of Them.** London, 1902.

16. L.C. Chiozza Money. **Riches and Poverty.** London, 1906.

17. Richard Mudie-Smith, Ed. **Handbook of the "Daily News" Sweated Industries' Exhibition.** London, 1906.

18. Edward Abbott Parry. **The Law and the Poor.** London, 1914.

19. Alexander Paterson. **Across the Bridges. Or Life by the South London River-side.** London, 1911.

20. M.S. Pember-Reeves. **Round About a Pound a Week.** London, 1913.

21. B. Seebohm Rowntree. **Poverty. A Study of Town Life.** London, 1910 (2nd ed.).

22. B. Seebohm Rowntree and Bruno Lasker. **Unemployment. A Social Study.** London, 1911.

23. B. Seebohm Rowntree and A.C. Pigou. **Lectures on Housing.** Manchester, 1914.

24. C.E.B. Russell. **Social Problems of the North.** London and Oxford, 1913.

25. Henry Solly. **Working Men's Social Clubs and Educational Institutes.** London, 1904.

26. E.J. Urwick, Ed. **Studies of Boy Life in Our Cities.** London, 1904.

27. Alfred Williams. **Life in a Railway Factory.** London, 1915.

28. [Women's Co-operative Guild]. **Maternity. Letters from Working-Women, Collected by the Women's Co-operative Guild with a preface by the Right Hon. Herbert Samuel, M.P.** London, 1915.

29. Women's Co-operative Guild. **Working Women and Divorce. An Account of Evidence Given on Behalf of the Women's Co-operative Guild before the Royal Commission on Divorce.** London, 1911.

   bound with Anna Martin. **The Married Working Woman. A Study.** London, 1911.